500
TIPS
on
GROUP
LEARNING

PHIL RACE

**KOGAN
PAGE**

London • Sterling (USA)

First published in 2000

Apart from any fair dealing for the purposes of research or private study, or criticism or review, as permitted under the Copyright, Designs and Patents Act 1988, this publication may only be reproduced, stored or transmitted, in any form or by any means, with the prior permission in writing of the publishers, or in the case of reprographic reproduction in accordance with the terms of licences issued by the Copyright Licensing Agency. Enquiries concerning reproduction outside those terms should be sent to the publishers at the undermentioned address:

Kogan Page Limited
120 Pentonville Road
London N1 9JN, UK
and
Stylus Publishing Inc.
22883 Quicksilver Drive
Sterling, VA 20166, USA

© Phil Race, 2000

British Library Cataloguing in Publication Data

A CIP record for this book is available from the British Library.

ISBN 0 7494 2884 8

Typeset by Jo Brereton, Primary Focus, Haslington, Cheshire
Printed and bound in Great Britain by Clays Ltd, St Ives plc

Contents

CONTENTS

Acknowledgements

I am grateful to the many group members, in my various workshops on teaching, learning and assessment over the years, from whom I learnt a great deal about the facilitation of group learning. Staff from the European Business School, London, the University of Durham and the London School of Hygiene and Tropical Medicine helped to brainstorm the ideas on 'damaging behaviours' in Chapter 5. I am particularly indebted to Sally Brown, whose work on group assessment is the basis of Chapter 6 of this book, and for several other contributions, notably on ways of forming groups, handling conflict, gender issues and for providing very useful feedback on draft versions of this book. I thank Steve McDowell for his permission to use ideas on virtual groups from our *500 Computing Tips for Trainers*, and Liz McDowell for her contribution on reflections on group work from *2000 Tips for Lecturers*. I also thank Abby Day and John Peters for permission to adapt extracts from our *500 Tips for Developing a Learning Organization*.

500 Tips from Kogan Page

500 Computing Tips for Teachers and Lecturers, 2nd Edition, Phil Race and Steve McDowell
500 Computing Tips for Trainers, Steve McDowell and Phil Race
500 ICT Tips for Primary Teachers, Steve Higgins, Nick Packard and Phil Race
500 Tips for Developing a Learning Organization, Phil Race, Abby Day and John Peters
500 Tips for Further and Continuing Education Lecturers, David Anderson, Sally Brown and Phil Race
500 Tips for Getting Published: a guide for educators, researchers and professionals, Dolores Black, Sally Brown, Abby Day and Phil Race
500 Tips for Open and Flexible Learning, Phil Race
500 Tips for Primary Teachers, Emma Packard, Nick Packard and Sally Brown
500 Tips for Quality Enhancement in Universities and Colleges, Sally Brown, Phil Race and Brenda Smith
500 Tips for Research Students, Sally Brown, Liz McDowell and Phil Race
500 Tips for School Improvement, Helen Horne and Sally Brown
500 Tips for Teachers, 2nd Edition, Sally Brown, Carolyn Earlam and Phil Race
500 Tips for TESOL, Sue Wharton and Phil Race
500 Tips for Trainers, Phil Race and Brenda Smith
500 Tips for Tutors, Phil Race and Sally Brown
500 Tips for Working with Children with Special Needs, Betty Vahid, Sally Harwood and Sally Brown
500 Tips on Assessment, Sally Brown, Phil Race and Brenda Smith

Foreword

Group learning is about getting people to work together well in carefully set up learning environments. The human species has evolved on the basis of group learning. Learning from other people is the most instinctive and natural of all the learning contexts we experience and starts at birth. Although learning can only be done by the learner, and can't be done 'to' the learner, the roles of other people in accelerating and modifying that learning are vitally important. Other people can enhance the quality of our learning and can also damage it. But which other people?

We hear much of collaborative learning as if it's the most natural activity in the world. But it often seems like the least natural, particularly amongst strangers. Sociological research tells us repeatedly that it is human nature not to be involved with people we don't know. We might make a mistake, or look stupid or be attacked. We will, however, get involved with people we do know. We'll help them with their problems and even defend them. The key to working and learning with other people is, therefore, the ability to lower barriers and become friends with would-be strangers, while acknowledging differences and respecting different viewpoints.

This book is about how to facilitate group learning. We explore what we as facilitators can do to overcome the human condition regarding collaboration, as well as identifying the things that are most likely to go wrong in group contexts, so that tactics can be found which will add up to a strategy for enabling successful group learning to happen.

Much of the literature on education and training has over the years concentrated on particular roles of the people who support learning, notably teachers, trainers and lecturers, and on the learning resources that are devised to assist learning, notably textbooks, handouts, computer-assisted learning packages and the Internet. It can be argued that in the quest to make teaching and training effective, and to design appropriate learning resource materials, the potential of people learning from each other has been somewhat neglected.

Now, at a time when buzz phrases include 'learning organizations', 'lifelong learning' and 'mass higher education', we need to face up to the importance of people learning from each other. Although sceptics will argue that most so-called learning organizations tend to be driven by the intended outcomes of the heads of organizations rather than of the individuals comprising them, and that lifelong learning is just another name for something that has always happened, the number of people who need to learn has grown in the rapidly changing world we now inhabit.

Furthermore, much is now said about transferable skills, or key skills, particularly oral communication skills, problem-solving skills, self-organization skills and reflection. Many of these skills can only be learnt from, and with, other people and cannot be developed solely by reading and studying what others have written about them. It is now increasingly accepted that the most important outcomes of education and training are about developing people, and not just what people know or understand. Employers and managers plead for employees who are able to work well with others and organize themselves. As the population of our planet increases, the need for people who can work well together is just as paramount as for people who can coexist together in general.

Group learning has never been as important as it is now. Yet we are still in a world where most teachers, educators and trainers are groomed in instruction rather than facilitation. This collection of practical suggestions is intended as one small step in adjusting the balance towards facilitation rather than training.

Despite the increased status of group learning, there is nothing fundamentally new in people learning together. Therefore, in this book, you will find at least as many ideas that you are already practising (or exceeding) as you will ideas that you have not tried out in your own work. Nevertheless, it is my hope that now and then you will find suggestions you can take and adapt, to add new impetus to those aspects of your own work about facilitating group learning.

Phil Race
January 2000

Chapter 1   Learning with others

Group learning involves two main kinds of processes – learning processes, and the processes of working with others. In this chapter, we start by taking a closer look at learning processes in general as well as in the particular context of collaborative learning. Suggestions are offered about ways of helping learners in groups to learn by doing, learn through feedback and learn from their mistakes, too. All of this depends at least to some extent on learners' levels of motivation – how strongly they want to learn and how well they have ownership of their need to learn.

The chapter ends with some suggestions on how to motivate group learners (and significant others in the overall picture of their learning) by expressing the benefits that can arise from successful group learning.

1

Learning about learning

Becoming better at learning is one of the most important aims for anyone participating in education or training programmes. To help people to be effective at learning in group situations, it is useful to help them to reappraise, if necessary, their thinking about how they learn best, so that they can take control of their learning processes consciously and develop them systematically. The following suggestions may help you to alert group learners to how they learn well.

1 **Remind people how long they've been learning to learn.** Ask them to reflect on just how much they actually learnt during the first two or three years of life. Remind them that most of this learning they did more or less under their own steam, without any conscious thought about teaching, training or even learning. Remind them that they still own the brain that did all of this, and can still use it to learn vast amounts of new knowledge, skills and competences.

2 **Ask people about their learning in school and college.** They will have learnt large amounts of information and will have forgotten most of it! However, they will have also learnt a great deal about how to take in knowledge and information and will still have this skill.

3 **Remind people that much of their real learning will have occurred in group situations.** While they will remember setting out systematically to learn some things on their own, the majority of their learning will have happened with other people around them.

4 **Remind people that they never stop learning to learn.** Ask people to think about some of the things that they have learnt only recently. Ask them how they learnt it. Ask them what they found out about themselves while learning it. Ask them who else was involved in one way or another during this learning.

5   **Provide programmes for people to learn about learning.** Training programmes can help people to tune into the power of their own minds. A good learning facilitator can help people to gain control of the processes by which they learn most efficiently, and how best they can use other people to help them to learn well. Many people find it useful to explore how their minds work in the company of other people and learn from each other's experiences.

6   **Provide resources to help people to learn about their own learning.** Not everyone is comfortable attending a training programme about learning to learn. Some people fear that inadequacies or deficiencies may be exposed. Computer-based or print-based packages that help people to explore their own learning in the comfort of privacy may be more attractive to such people. Such packages can also help people to reflect on the differences between learning alone and learning with others.

7   **Get people asking themselves, 'What did I learn about myself when I learnt this?'** Learning to learn is closely connected with understanding one's own mind and one's own preferences and choices. Suggest that people learn even more about themselves when they reflect on group interactions.

8   **Get people asking, 'What really worked when I learnt this?'** The chances are that the factors that made one element of learning successful will be transferable to their next element of learning. There are long words for this, such as 'metacognitive processing', but it's simply about helping people to be looking inwards at what works for them when they learn and what doesn't. In particular, it is useful to get people thinking about what works best for them in group situations so that they can help to make learning groups more productive.

9   **Get people teasing out what slows their learning down.** The more we all know about how the brakes work, the better we can use them only when we need them. In the context of group learning, it is helpful for all group members to be aware of the things that can interfere with effective collaborative learning so that they can minimize such effects.

10   **Legitimize learning to learn in the appraisal cycle.** If your organization uses regular appraisal or review interviews, include the agenda of what people have learnt about their own learning since the last interview, and ask them to comment on how much of this learning was in group contexts.

11 **Get individuals to articulate 'learning to learn' targets.** Target-setting should not just be about gaining further knowledge, competences or skills, but should include setting out goals relating to the further development of a learning toolkit of approaches and methods. When individuals have defined their targets already, it is much quicker for a group to start off by finding out how many of these targets are congruent.

2

Group learning means learning by doing

'One must learn by doing the thing; though you think you know it, you have no certainty until you try' (Sophocles, 495–406 BC). A lot has been said (and written) about how human beings learn most effectively. Psychology is still a very young science! Some of the theories and models are more easily related to practice than others. It is worth asking people who are about to learn in group contexts how they became good at something, comparing their answers with each other's and with the responses given below, and then following up the implications of people's answers to these questions. This will help you to find out more about how to help people to learn effectively together.

1   **Think of something that you know you do well.** How did you become good at this? Most people reply with words such as: 'Lots of practice', 'I learnt this by doing it', 'I became good at this through trial and error'. Seeing the common ground in their answers to these questions can help group learners to see how they can learn well collaboratively.

2   **Avoid pigeonholing people into 'learning styles'.** While there is much to be gained in alerting people to their preferred ways of learning, there is a serious danger that they end up feeling that they are trapped in the styles that they seem to have adopted for themselves. Human beings are very versatile animals, and can change their approaches to learning much more easily than is sometimes suggested.

3   **Cater for learning by doing by groups.** This is sometimes called 'experiential learning'. If you intend people to become skilled, competent or knowledgeable about something, by far the fastest and most efficient way is to get them to have a go, together, at whatever is involved. The task briefings for group learning are vitally important.

4   **Reading is not necessarily doing!** Don't assume that if you provide people with information (print-based or electronic) that they will automatically be able to learn from it just by reading it. While reading may be a key step, it is essential that they do things to apply and try out what they read – every bit of the way along the learning curve – not just at the end of it.

5   **Listening to experts is little to do with doing!** Lectures and training programmes often involve too much of trainees listening to experts. Knowledge and skills do not enter people's minds through their ears. A small amount of listening needs to be followed quickly by an episode of learning by doing.

6   **Listening to each other has a lot to do with effective group learning.** We all try to deal sensitively with situations involving people who are 'hard of hearing', but it takes much greater skill to deal with those who are 'hard of listening'. Alert group members to this issue.

7   **Make it possible for people to practise sufficiently.** Repetition counts a lot in learning by doing. Repetition helps people to build up speed and this helps them to develop confidence. When someone has practised something several times, they become more competent and proficient at doing it and have to think less about how to go about it successfully. Group learning is an ideal context for practice.

8   **Make it OK to get things wrong at first.** Learning from one's mistakes is a healthy, natural and productive way of learning. The art of helping people to learn from their mistakes lies in setting the scene for them to make mistakes in a comfortable, blame-free environment. Design safe practice opportunities for people to learn, and try to ensure that learning groups avoid a blame culture.

9   **Choose learning resources that keep learning active.** Interactive open or flexible learning packages can give people the learning by doing practice that they need, whereas textbooks or manuals may merely provide them with the information that they need. Learning is about using and applying information, not just storing it up in one's memory. Resource-based group learning needs to be about working collaboratively with resources, not just allocating individual tasks to group members.

10 **Retain some degree of the comfort of privacy in which to make mistakes.** Where people can have a go at something under conditions where no one else sees them get it wrong, they are better able to learn comfortably from mistakes. Learning resources that have self-assessment tasks and exercises make good use of this principle, and allow people to find out about their own mistakes in the comfort of privacy and to avoid making them when other people would notice them.

11 **Think about the differences between training and teaching.** A good trainer gets trainees learning by doing and facilitates their learning. Teachers tend to try to 'deliver' information, experience and wisdom, but there's not too much chance of it being received successfully. Turn your teachers into good trainers.

3

Group learning means learning through feedback

Learning is a natural human process. Human beings are creatures with feelings. Most human beings are social animals and have feelings about each other as well as about anything they are learning. It is worth exploring how feelings affect the quality of learning. The following suggestions can help you to tease out the importance of the role of feedback in helping people, who are learning together, to develop positive feelings about their progress.

1   **Legitimize feelings.** In some cultures, people tend to hide from their feelings or to try not to let their feelings show. In group learning contexts, failing to confront and to work with human feelings can set up unnecessary barriers and defences and can undermine the potential of the group.

2   **Ask people to identify something they feel good about.** This can be a positive attribute in their own make-up, or an aspect of their personality in which they have a sense of pride. It can also be something that they have learnt that they feel pride in. Don't embarrass them by asking them what it is, but instead then ask them the next question.

3   **Ask them what evidence they have to support their positive feelings.** Most people are likely to reply along the following lines: 'Other people's reactions', 'Feedback from other people', 'Seeing the results'. Point out the importance of feedback from other people in helping to develop positive feelings, and the consequent importance of feedback in successful group learning.

4   **Get people in pairs to think of a compliment about each other.** Then get them to say it to each other. They are quite likely to laugh. Ask them why they did so. They are likely to use words such as: 'I was embarrassed'. Point out that they have just done something that is likely to be directly contrary to their responses to question 3 above, and (in admittedly a pleasant way) that they have in effect rejected some positive feedback and devalued the potential benefit to them of the feedback.

5   **Suggest that people try giving each other a compliment, this time thanking each other for the feedback.** Help them to see that by accepting the feedback rather than shrugging it off as unimportant they have opened the door to further positive feedback, and have used the feedback to improve their feelings about whatever might have been involved. Explain how the process of helping people to accept positive feedback can contribute strongly to effective group learning.

6   **Ask people to think of some critical feedback about each other!** Then, if you dare, ask them to articulate this feedback and to thank each other for it. Point out how this is the other side of the picture, and that critical feedback can also be very valuable in group learning, but only if it is accepted graciously and then analysed and considered. Also point out the dangers of shrugging off useful feedback by adopting a defensive stance and effectively closing the door to any further critical feedback being offered.

7   **Ask people to think of ways that they can deliberately seek out feedback from each other.** Remind them that it may be up to them as individuals to open the doors both for positive and critical feedback, and that the more feedback they solicit the greater they can make rational and constructive use of it. Draw out the connections between a group climate or culture of free exchange of feedback and cumulative effective learning.

8   **Ask people to reflect upon the various processes through which they can obtain feedback.** Help them to explore their own preferences for face-to-face feedback, written feedback, first-hand feedback and second-hand feedback.

9   **Get people thinking about how they can keep track of the feedback they receive and their follow-up actions.** Help them to realize that feedback is only really useful if they turn it into action and development. Suggest ways for group members to keep a record of both positive and critical feedback, and link this to action planning and further evaluation of their actions.

10   **Help people to work out how they can keep track of the effects of feedback that they give to others.** It can be valuable to follow up positive feedback that they have given, to make sure that the recipients have really allowed themselves to grow from it and take it fully on board.

4

Things going wrong can be good group learning

'An expert is a man who has made all the mistakes, which can be made, in a very narrow field' (Niels Bohr, physicist, 1885 1962). Learning from trial and error is a perfectly valid way to learn. Learning from mistakes is how most people learn many important things. Obviously, it is important to protect group learners from any serious consequences of learning from their mistakes, but this is usually quite feasible to arrange. The following suggestions may help you to turn 'mistakes' into a valuable pathway towards successful group learning.

1   **Ask people to think of something that they are not good at.** Ask them to explore why they think that they have not become good at whatever it is. Ask them to work out what might have gone wrong in their learning for such an element of their life. Allow group members then to see how much they are likely to have in common regarding learning from things that went wrong.

2   **Remind people that problems are bonding opportunities.** When members of a group have a problem to solve, it can bring them closer together than if things had worked out without there ever having been any problems.

3   **Help people to sort out any 'self-blame' aspects.** People are very likely to take the blame onto themselves. They are quite likely to link their lack of success to personal deficiencies in their approaches to learning. Ask them to go a little further and to work out whether what went wrong can be tracked down to their actions (or the lack of particular actions) rather than to their personalities or natures. It usually can!

4   **Ask people to think further about someone else being to blame.** Ask them to move beyond blaming particular people and to look instead at the actions that these people took (or did not take). Help them to see how much better it is to concentrate on analysing actions than to think negatively about personalities, and to distance their thoughts about what people are from their analysis of what people do. Remind them that it is much easier to cause changes in what people do than in what people are. Confronting the concept of blame in this way can help groups to set out to avoid a blame culture.

5   **Help to talk people away from the concept of blame.** While it can be useful to pin down the causes of things that go wrong to actions, or to lack of actions, it is best to distance these actions from the people who were involved.

6   **Get people to think about the real value of learning from things that went wrong.** Ask them to work out whether their learning from mistakes may have turned out to be deeper and more enduring than their learning from successes. Prompt people to view things that go wrong as potentially valuable learning experiences. Suggest that this can be a key value in group learning, and can help all experiences to deliver their maximum benefit to everyone concerned.

7   **Exploit the power of games and simulations.** These can provide safe circumstances for learning collaboratively important skills through trial and error. It is worth designing particular simulations to provide people with the opportunity to practise their reactions to difficult real life circumstances, so that when they meet them for real they are better able to tackle them confidently.

8   **Play with negative brainstorming.** Anticipate things that could go wrong in a learning group, and get people to brainstorm as many ways as they can think of that could make them go wrong more badly and more quickly. Often, doing the reverse may help to prevent things from going wrong in the first place, and the advance thinking may be useful when something is noticed that could lead to a problem.

9   **Capture things that actually go wrong.** Turn these into case studies with which to train other people, so that the lessons learnt from unfortunate group happenings are translated more widely into the experience base available to learning groups.

10 **Advocate the value of unconditional positive regard for people.** Even when it may be necessary in learning groups for members to be critical of each other's actions, it remains possible (and highly desirable) to value and approve of the people themselves. Use examples in your own experience about how well people respond to feeling valued and how this can make fast and dramatic changes to their actions.

5

Group learning means motivation... wanting to learn...

One indicator of a healthy learning group is a general ethos where people *want* to learn. This is sometimes called 'intrinsic motivation', but the straightforward word *want* is more powerful. Incentives such as money or promotion can help people to want to learn, but this is really 'extrinsic motivation', and it is even better if the want to learn comes from inside people. The following suggestions may help you to fuel group members' want to learn.

1   **Get people thinking about, 'What's in it for me to learn this collabora-tively?'** Group learning requires the investment of time and energy, and it would be unreasonable to expect people to put their hearts into it unless they can see some reason to make it worth their while.

2   **Ask people who are already learning well collaboratively why it works for them.** You may be surprised by the rich diversity of motivations that fire different people. The more you find out about what keeps successfully motivated people learning in groups, the more you can spread some of their motivators to other people.

3   **Get people to upgrade their reasons for learning in groups.** Sometimes, people are learning out of a vague sense that they should be doing so or because the groups have been set up for them. Help them to find more tangible reasons for striving to learn well collaboratively, so that when the learning becomes more difficult they have something stronger to keep them going.

4   **Establish personal ownership for wanting to learn.** Different reasons for learning fire different people. It is best when everyone in a learning group feels a sense of ownership over their own rationale for learning in the group. Sometimes people may have quite unique or even strange reasons for learning, but so long as their reasons work for them, this is fine.

5   **Get people to work out their own intended learning outcomes for group learning.** Help them to be specific and realistic. Help them to set sensible timescales for each learning outcome. Help them to structure their planned learning into manageable steps.

6   **Suggest to people that they make their intentions public!** Telling other people about one's planned learning outcomes can help us to achieve them – we prefer not to be found not to have lived up to our plans. It can be particularly useful to let other members of a learning group in on planned personal targets and deadlines – they can then offer a significant driving force.

7   **Channel group members' motivation into learning by doing.** If people want to make sure that their learning is active, they are much less likely to fall into learning limbo, and will be watching the learning payoff that they are deriving from each part of their learning processes.

8   **Help group members to want to learn from feedback.** Feedback is a vital process for successful learning, and it is worth getting people to develop a thirst for feedback, rather than just being content with using it when it happens to be received. People who are seeking out feedback are able to learn much more quickly, by adjusting their approach continuously rather than occasionally.

9   **Encourage people to want to digest what they learn.** Making sense of complex ideas does not always happen easily, but when people are trying together to make sense of them it is more likely to happen. Remind people, however, that some things take their own time to digest, and that it is often possible to be perfectly competent at doing something without yet being able to understand it.

10 **Get people in learning groups to look back at their successful learning.** Help them to celebrate their successes. Help them to explore how their learning was successful, and to capture what they have learnt about their own approaches so that they can harness this to make their next episode of group learning even more successful.

... or needing to learn

There are times when, with the best will in the world, it is hard to want to learn a particular thing! Then, some other kind of motivation may be needed. The following suggestions may help you to assist people to discover alternative driving forces for their group learning.

1   **Ask people about what kept them going in the past.** Ask them to think of something they did not really want to learn but kept on and did, in fact, learn successfully. Ask them, 'What kept you at it?' Many of the same driving forces may continue to be available for future learning. The remainder of this set of tips is based on some of the most common driving forces that can keep group members investing in their collaborative learning.

2   **Necessity is the mother of much learning.** When people can see why it would be useful for them to learn something, it can help them to invest the time and energy that it will take. Try to get group members thinking for themselves about how the learning in question will serve them well. When they have ownership of their need to learn something, they are much more likely to try to learn it.

3   **Get group members to look to beyond their learning.** Learning can often provide a passport to opportunities that would otherwise be unavailable to them. Even when there may be no immediate intention to go for the opportunities, it is attractive to have the option.

4   **Strong, positive human support fuels learning.** When people have a lot of encouragement, they don't usually want to let down their sponsors or backers. Ideally, this strong support can come not only from fellow members of a learning group, but also from other people beyond the group.

5   **People like to be praised and celebrated.** Many a learner has kept going, when the going got tough, by thinking ahead to the moment of glory when success would be celebrated, perhaps with them being presented with an award or a degree. Remind group members of the rewards, especially when they are tackling difficult learning.

6

Behaviours of a good leader

Much has been written about the qualities and attributes associated with effective leadership. It all, however, boils down to what leaders actually do. The following list of 'good leader behaviours' (not presented in any significant order here) can be used as a starting point for groups working out who will lead and how.

A good leader:

- doesn't confuse leadership with control and invites participation from all group members;
- earns the respect of other group members;
- notices when someone feels like an outsider and tactfully draws them in;
- shows no favouritism to individual group members and treats them as having equal potential;
- gets to know the strengths and weaknesses of group members and apportions workload accordingly;
- keeps an eye on group dynamics and defuses conflict before it gets out of hand;
- is always there, particularly at the start of group meetings;
- knows when to keep quiet and let others take the initiative;
- makes space for lateral thinking and off-the-wall ideas, which may seem weird at first, but may enrich later thinking;
- allows group members to have ownership of their own best ideas;
- has the tact to guide choices without leaving those whose ideas were rejected feeling let down;
- finds something of value to commend even in the least able group member and is unstinting in praise for those who contribute a great deal;

- is sensitive to issues of gender, race and age and makes sure that no one feels disadvantaged or excluded because of such factors;
- doesn't leap automatically to what seems the most obvious solution, but allows diverse views to be expressed and considered;
- has an active brief to ensure equivalence of contribution for group members and that everyone feels they are being treated fairly;
- undertakes effective project planning, with built-in milestones and check points, to ensure that the group's task is achieved;
- keeps referring back to the task brief to ensure that work is productive and on target;
- sets SMART goals for the group, which are specific, measurable, achievable, realistic and time-specific;
- has an ever watchful eye for the evidence that will show that the group will have achieved its intended objectives;
- manages group resources (including any project budget) carefully to ensure that targets are achieved;
- has contingency plans for when things go wrong;
- admits own mistakes and shares responsibility when these cause the group's work to go off target;
- doesn't automatically blame others when things go wrong (unless it is genuinely caused by destructive or lazy behaviour of others);
- knows how to delegate effectively without making group members feel that they have been dumped on;
- puts as much energy into making sure that the group process works as into contributing towards generating the ultimate product;
- knows when to seek outside help and when the group can continue autonomously;
- is methodical about ensuring that good records are kept of group meetings and delegated activities;
- ensures at the end of each group session that other participants are clear about when and where the next session will take place;
- clarifies for the group members exactly what each individual is expected to do prior to the next meeting;
- makes sure that when the group process ends there is a sense of closure with a final 'washing-up' meeting and, if appropriate, some kind of celebration.

7

Group learning includes following

Leadership is often discussed in the context of group work, but it can be argued that 'followership' is just as important. Group learning is an ideal context to help all kinds of people to develop and practise leadership skills, but there will always need to be more followers than leaders. We all know the problems that occur when too many people try to lead a group! The suggestions below may help you to ensure that your leaders have skilled followers. They may also help to optimize the learning that can be achieved through well thought out following.

1   **Brief groups about the importance of followership.** It can be important to legitimize followership as a vital factor to underpin the success of group work.

2   **Explain that followership should not be regarded as weakness.** When leadership is rotating between group members, they should regard their work when not leading as every bit as important as when they are directing the actions of the group.

3   **Accept that followership requires well-developed skills and attributes.** For example, patience may be needed. When it takes a little time for the purpose or wisdom of a leadership decision to become apparent, it is sometimes harder to wait for this to happen than to jump in and try to steer the group or argue with the decision.

4   **More followers than leaders are needed!** It is virtually impossible to have a successful group where all members are adopting leading stances at the same time. Although the credit for successful group work is often attributed to the leader, it is often the followers who actually own the success. It is more than good sense to acknowledge this right from the start of any group work situation.

5   **Followership is a valuable, transferable key skill.** In all walks of life, people need to be followers at least for some of the time. It can be useful to employ group work situations to help people to develop skills that will make them good followers in other contexts of their lives and careers.

6   **Good followership is not the same as being 'easily led'.** Being 'easily led' is taken usually to imply that people are led into doing things against their better judgement. Good followership is closer to being easily led when the direction of the task in hand coincides quite closely to the individual's own judgement.

7   **Followership should not be blind obedience!** Encourage group members to think about how they are following, why they are following, for how long they are going to be content with following and what they are learning through following.

8   **Suggest that group members experiment with a 'followership log'.** This could be private notes to themselves of their experiences of being led, but it is more important to make notes on their feelings as followers than to write down criticisms of the actions of the leaders. Whether the logs are treated as private or shared notes can be decided later by everyone involved in a group.

9   **Legitimize followership notes as authentic evidence of the operation of a group.** Such notes can tell their own stories regarding the relative contributions of members of the group, the group processes that worked well and those that worked badly. When it is known that followership records will count towards the evidence of achievement of a group, leadership itself is often done more sensitively and effectively.

10 **Followership is vital training for leadership.** People who have been active, reflective followers can bring their experience of followership to bear on their future leadership activities. Having consciously reflected on the experience of following informs leadership approaches and makes their own leadership easier for others to follow.

11 **Good followership is partly about refraining from nit-picking.** When people have too strong a desire to promote their individuality, it often manifests itself in the form of expending energy in trying to achieve unimportant minor adjustments to the main processes going on in group work. Good followership involves adopting restraint about minor quibbles, and saving interventions for those occasions where it is important not to follow without question.

8

Benefits of group learning

There are countless benefits associated with successful group learning. One way of identifying benefits is to address the question, 'What's in it for me?' There are several different target audiences for these benefits, including:

- learners (and prospective learners) themselves;
- tutors, trainers, and learning facilitators;
- employers, or future employers of learners;
- learning organizations and institutions.

The following benefits messages may give you a starting point to 'sell' the concept of group learning to each of these respective target audiences. Each benefits message is intended to explain, to the people needing convincing about group learning, what's in it for them. The messages therefore are written directly to learners, tutors, employers and organizational managers, in the language that they are most likely to warm to.

Benefits for group learners themselves

Group learning means that you:

1 **Have a more enjoyable, sociable learning experience.** You will already know that learning on your own can become tedious and that other people can become distractions from your learning. With group learning, other people actually help your learning to be more successful.

2 **Make new friends.** It's useful to have at least some of your friends from among the people studying alongside you. You never know when you may need their help, such as if you're ill and have to miss a session. Many learners find studying with friends so useful that they set up their own learning syndicates, and practise group learning by themselves to their mutual advantage.

3   **Get much more feedback on how your learning is going.** Working with fellow learners helps you to see where you stand. You can tell more easily whether you're ahead of the game or lagging behind, in which case you can do something about it. Feedback from tutors or trainers is still valuable, of course, but you get a lot more feedback when you're working with people rather than after you've done something and submitted it for assessment.

4   **Receive better explanations of things you don't understand.** When fellow learners explain something to you, they are likely to be able to explain it better than someone who has understood it for a long time. Fellow learners will still remember exactly how the light dawned for them and can help the light to dawn for you, too.

5   **Learn a lot by explaining things to fellow learners.** When you explain something to a fellow learner who doesn't yet understand it, it's actually you that gets the most out of it. Putting something into words to help someone else to understand it forces you to get a much better grip on it yourself, and your own learning becomes much deeper and more permanent.

6   **Pick up useful skills which employers value.** Group learning is the ideal way to practise your oral communication skills as well as to develop your ability to work in teams. You can practise leadership roles, and (even more importantly sometimes) get better at letting other people lead the group as well.

7   **Gather evidence for your CV.** Ideally, your CV should present a picture not just of a successful learner, but of a well-rounded person who is more than able to get on with other people in a variety of different circumstances. Records of what you have achieved through group learning help to portray you as a successful person, not just a successful learner.

Benefits for tutors, trainers, learning facilitators

Group learning means that you:

1   **Have some of the pressure taken away from you.** When learners do at least some of their studying collaboratively, it gives you time to plan what *you* are going to do next with them or simply to take a break from leading the group.

2   **Have learners who aren't so dependent upon you.** This means that when some of them are having problems getting to grips with an idea or topic, it isn't entirely up to you to help them to sort it out.

3   **Have learners who are more likely to be successful.** When group learning is working well, it tends to help both the weaker learners and the stronger ones, and all of this means that your own standing as a successful facilitator is increased.

4   **Spend much less time explaining the same things to different learners.** The things you're most often called upon to explain are likely to be ones that learners in groups can explain to each other. This helps them to deepen their learning more than if they were simply to have you, an expert, explain it to them.

5   **Can devote your energies to the most important problems.** The things that a group of learners can't sort out for themselves are likely to be the ones where they really need your expertise. This means less time for you explaining routine or straightforward things to individuals.

6   **Can learn more from your learners.** Individuals may be too shy or embarrassed to discuss matters arising from their learning easily with you, but in learning groups they can be much more open with each other. You'll often find when eavesdropping on a group discussion that you're alerted to things that would not have come to light if learners were working on their own.

7   **Can make your sessions with learners more interesting.** For example, getting different groups of learners to look at different sides of a story or scenario can make it more interesting for everyone when small groups come back to share their decisions or findings. Also, you'll have more opportunity to offer learners some choice about which aspects of a problem or issue their group will explore.

8   **Find out more about your learners.** Watching learners working together always tells you important things about their individual personalities. This will often help you to understand them better as individuals and to adjust your own approach to them. Sometimes, this additional information will be important, such as when you're asked to write a reference for a learner.

9   **Find out more about your colleagues.** Discussing group learning is often easier than discussing lecturing or training, as group learning is in itself less of a private activity. This means that you may find colleagues more forthcoming to exchange with you their experiences of working with groups than other aspects of their work.

10   **Can save a lot of time and energy when assessing.** For example, involving groups of learners in peer-assessing each other's work can deepen their own learning as well as save you time. It can be much quicker to moderate a batch of work that has already been peer-assessed than to assess it yourself from scratch.

Benefits for employers (or future employers) of learners

Group learning means that you:

1   **Are likely to have your staff trained in useful transferable skills.** People who have done a lot of group learning are likely to develop communication skills, interpersonal skills and confidence, all of which are valuable attributes in employees.

2   **Are likely to be able to make better appointment decisions.** Group learning helps people to come across more naturally at interview, and this helps you to select the most suitable candidates.

3   **Gain employees who will continue to work collaboratively.** Most jobs require at least some degree of team playing and some jobs vitally depend on it. Experience in group learning means that your employees are not having to learn their team playing skills from scratch.

4   **Gain staff who are less dependent on supervision.** Good experience of group learning helps to develop people's autonomy and self-reliance. This can make the task of supervising them or managing them a lot easier (unless, of course, you're really searching for people who will simply do what they're told to do).

5   **Get staff who know themselves better.** One of the most significant benefits of group learning is that people find out a lot about their own behaviours and attitudes. The better people know themselves, the better you can find out how to make good use of their talents.

6   **Get staff who are better at problem solving and decision making.** Group learning is an ideal training ground for these skills, as learners can experiment with different approaches and learn from each other's solutions.

Benefits for learning organizations and institutions

It is, of course, impossible to express benefits directly to an institution or organization, so this time the benefits are addressed to senior managers.

Group learning means that your organization:

1   **Will be all the more successful because people work well together.** Group learning helps people to be good collaborators rather than competitors. It's fine for groups to compete in a healthy way, but not so good for individuals to be watching their own backs all the time.

2   **(If you're a learning institution), is less dependent on the expertise of your teachers or trainers.** Group learning means that people can learn a lot from each other and not so much depends on direct teaching or training.

3   **Will perform better when subjected to external scrutiny.** Any external reviewer of teaching quality is likely to be more impressed by successful collaborative activities between learners, than simply by watching straight teaching taking place. Such people are usually briefed to look for successful interaction as a basis for learning.

4   **Will turn out learners who are more employable.** The reputation of any learning organization depends on the people who come from it. If your organization gets known as a source of people who can work well collaboratively as well as individually, your learners will be more sought after and, in turn, this can attract more prestige for the organization itself.

Chapter 2   Getting groups going

There are no second chances to get groups off to a good start. The first few minutes of the lifetime of any group can set precedents and establish the atmosphere in ways that are difficult or impossible to reverse. The suggestions in this chapter are intended as a starting point, from which to select and adapt the ideas that make most sense in the context of your own group learning contexts. The earlier sections of this chapter relate particularly to groups where the overt agenda is learning together, and where the groups may be set up deliberately rather than formed in an *ad hoc* fashion. The last four sections broaden the scope and relate more directly to spontaneous groups in charge of their own agenda.

9

Preparing learners for group work

Learners often feel that they are competing with each other and need considerable encouragement to relax such feelings and begin to work collaboratively and effectively. The following suggestions include a first look at several aspects of group learning and are expanded upon in later parts of this book.

1   **Help learners to understand the benefits of being able to work together in groups.** Explain to learners that there are real skills to be gained from group work tasks, and that the ability to contribute effectively to teams that they will develop is important to employers.

2   **Think about the different ways of forming groups.** These include forming groups randomly, using alphabetical lists, or forming groups on the basis of background, interest or ability, or allowing learners to choose their own group compositions. Each method has its own advantages and drawbacks. The best compromise is to rotate group membership and to ensure that learners are not 'stuck' in the same group for too long, especially if it does not have a successful dynamic.

3   **Think about the optimum group size for the group tasks you have in mind for learners.** The most suitable group size will differ according to the nature of the task. Pairs are ideal for some tasks, while for other kinds of group work threes, fours or fives are better. If the group is larger than about six, individuals tend to opt out or feel unable to make useful contributions to the group.

4   **Give learners some training in group processes.** It can be useful to use an icebreaker with the whole class, during which learners work for a short while in groups. They are then briefed to analyse exactly what went well and what didn't work in the group episode, and to identify reasons for good and bad processes.

5   **Structure learners' early attempts at group work.** It can be helpful to provide quite detailed lists of briefing instructions, and to ask each group to allocate the tasks among the members. This can be useful for helping groups to work out their own directions, and then allocate them fairly in future group work.

6   **Help learners to understand the reasons why group work can go wrong.** The more learners know about the things that work, and the hazards of interpersonal relationships and group dynamics, the better they can cope with the aspects of human nature that inevitably play their part in any kind of group situation.

7   **Ensure that there are suitable places for learners to work in groups.** Make sure that there are places where learners can talk, argue and discuss things, and not just in whispers in an area that is supposed to be kept quiet. It is also useful if the group work venues are such that learners are not being observed or overheard by their tutors, or by any other groups, at least for some of the time that they work together.

8   **Give learners support and guidance when things go wrong.** It is not enough just to criticize a group where processes have failed; learners need advice on what to do to rectify the situation and how to handle disagreements or conflicts successfully.

9   **Be fair and firm with assessment.** Always ensure that each individual's contributions are fairly measured and assessed. Don't allow learners to think that they will all earn the same mark, even if they have not all made equal contributions to the work of the group. Logs of meetings, breakdowns of who agreed to do what and evidence of the contributions members brought to the group, can all be prepared by learners and can all lend themselves to assessment at the end of the group work.

10 **Get learners to evaluate the effectiveness of their group work.** Including such an evaluation as an assessed element in each learner's work can cause all of the members of a group to reflect on the processes involved in their working together, and to deepen their learning about the processes involved in effective team working.

10

Ways of forming groups

There are many different ways in which you can create groups of students from a larger class. All have their own advantages and disadvantages. It is probably best to use a mixture of methods, so that students experience a healthy level of variety of group composition to maximize the benefits of learning from and with each other.

1   **Friendship groups.** Allowing students to arrange themselves into groups has the advantage that most groups feel a sense of ownership regarding their composition. However, there are often some students 'left over' in the process and they can feel alienated through not having been chosen by their peers. Friendship groups may also differ quite widely in ability level, as high-fliers select to work with like-minded students.

2   **Geographical groups.** Simply putting students into groups according to clusters as they are already sitting (or standing) in the larger group is one of the easiest and quickest ways of dividing a class into groups. This is likely to include some friendship groups in any case, but minimizes the embarrassment of some students who might not have been selected in a friendship group. The ability distribution may, however, be skewed as it is not unusual for the students nearest the tutor to be rather higher in motivation compared to those in the most remote corner of the room!

3   **Alphabetical (family name) groups.** This is one of several random ways of allocating group membership. It is easy to achieve if you already have an alphabetical class list. However, it can happen that students often find themselves in the same group if several tutors use the same process of group selection. Also, when working with multicultural large classes, several students from the same culture may have the same family name, and some groups may end up dominated by one culture, which may not be what you intend to happen.

4   **Other alphabetical groups.** For example, you can form groups on the basis of the last letter of students' first names. This is likely to make a refreshing change from family name alphabetical arrangements. Students also get off to a good start in seeing each other's first names at the outset.

5   **Number groups.** When students are given a number (for example, on a class list), you can easily arrange for different combinations of groups for successive tasks by selecting a variety of number permutations (including using a random number generator if you have one on your computer). Groups of four could be '1-4, 5-8, ...' for task 1, then '1,3,5,7, 2,4,6,8, ...', then '1, 5, 9, 13', and so on.

6   **Class list rotating syndicates.** Suppose you had 24 students in a class and on an overhead transparency you printed their names. You could draw separate columns down the list for successive group tasks, for example starting with 'A,A,A,A, B,B,B,B...', then 'A,B,C,D A,B,C,D...', then 'A,B,C,D,E,F, A,D,C,D,E,F to split them respectively into different groups of four, and groups of six.

7   **Astrological groups.** When selecting group membership from a large class, it makes a change to organize the selection on the basis of calendar month of birth date. Similarly, 'star signs' could be used – but not all students know when (for example) Gemini starts and finishes in the year. This method often leads to groups of somewhat different sizes, however, and you may have to engineer some transfers if equal group size is needed. Participants from some religions may also find the method bizarre or inappropriate.

8   **Crossovers.** When you wish to systematically share the thinking of one group with another, you can ask one person from each group to move to another group. For example, you can ask the person with the earliest birthday in the year to move to the next group clockwise round the room, carrying forward the product or notes from the previous group and introducing the thinking behind that to the next group. The next exchange could be the person with the latest birthday, and so on. When doing this, you need to make sure that not too many students end up stuck in the same physical position for too long.

9   **Coded name labels.** Give out self-adhesive labels for students to write their names on, but with a series of codes already on the labels. A three-digit code of a Greek letter, normal letter, and a number can lead to the possibility of all students finding themselves in three completely different groups for successive tasks. Six of each letters and numbers allows an overall group of 36 students to split into different sixes three times, for example, with each student working cumulatively with 17 other students.

10   **Performance-related groups.** Sometimes you may wish to set out to balance the ability range in each group, for example, by including one high-flier and one low-flier in each group. The groups could then be constituted on the basis of the last marked assignment or test. Alternatively, it can be worth occasionally setting a task where all high-fliers and all low-fliers are put into the same group, with most of the groups randomly middle-fliers, but this (although appreciated by the high-fliers) can be divisive to overall morale.

11   **Skills-based groups.** For some group tasks (especially fairly extended ones), it can be worthwhile to try to arrange that each group has at least one member with identified skills and competences (for example, doing a Web search, using a word-processing package, leading a presentation, and so on). A short questionnaire can be issued to the whole class, asking students to self-rate themselves on a series of skills, and groups can be constituted on the basis of these.

12   **Hybrid groups.** You may wish to organize learners by ability or in learning teams, and may at the same time wish to help them to avoid feeling that they are isolated from everyone they already know. In this case, you can ask each of them to nominate a partner they would like to work with, then group the pairs as you feel most appropriate.

11

Group size considerations

Helping students (and colleagues) to maximize the benefits of collaborative working depends quite significantly on choice of group size. This needs to be appropriate to the tasks involved as well as to the nature of the individuals constituting the group. Each group size possibility brings its own advantages and disadvantages. The following comments and suggestions on particular group sizes may help you to plan the composition of groups.

1   **Pairs.** It is usually relatively easy to group students in twos – either by choosing the pairs yourself, random methods or friendship pairs. Advantages include a low probability of passenger behaviour and the relative ease in which a pair can arrange meeting schedules. Problems can occur when pairs fall out.

2   **Couples.** In any class of students, there are likely to be some established couples. When they work together on collaborative work, the chances are that they will put a lot more into group work than ordinary pairs, not least because they are likely to spend more time and energy on the tasks involved. The risks include the possibility of the couple becoming destabilized, which can make further collaborative work much more difficult for them.

3   **Threes.** Trios represent a very popular group size. The likelihood of passenger behaviours is quite low, and trios will often work well together sharing out tasks appropriately. It is easier for trios to arrange meetings schedules than for larger groups. The most likely problem is for two of the students to work together better than with the third, who can gradually (or suddenly) become, or feel, marginalized.

4   **Fours.** This is still quite small as a group size. Passenger behaviour is possible, but less likely than in larger groups. When subdividing group tasks, it can be useful to split into pairs for some activities and work as individuals for others. There are three different ways that a quartet can subdivide into pairs, adding variety to successive task distribution possibilities.

5   **Fives.** The possibility of passenger behaviour begins to increase significantly now, and it becomes more important for the group to have a leader for each stage of its work. However, because of the odd number, there is usually the possibility of a casting vote when making decisions, rather than the group being stuck equally divided regarding a choice of action. There are many ways that a group of five can subdivide into twos and threes, allowing variety in the division of tasks among its members.

6   **Sixes.** The possibility of passenger behaviour is yet more significant and group leadership is more necessary. The group can, however, subdivide into threes or twos in many different ways. It is now much more difficult to ensure equivalence of tasks for group members.

7   **More than six.** Such groups are less likely to be suitable for group or team tasks, but can still be useful for discussion and debate before splitting into smaller groups for action. Passengers may be able to avoid making real contributions to the work of the group and can find themselves outcasts because of this.

8   **Even larger groups...** When it is necessary to set up working groups that are much larger than six, the role of the leader needs to change considerably. A skilled facilitator is needed to get a large group collaborating well. It can be advantageous for the facilitator to become somewhat neutral, and to concentrate on achieving consensus and agreement rather than attempting to set the direction of the group.

9   **Playing to strengths.** A group can reach targets faster and more efficiently by choosing to use the identified strengths of each of its members when subdividing tasks and roles. The learning payoff, however, is less than when playing to weaknesses (see below). When the overall product of the group is being assessed, groups tend to play to strengths.

10 **Playing to weaknesses.** A group that chooses to play to identified weaknesses is using one of the most effective ways to develop skills and attitudes of its members. The members of the group with identified strengths can set out to help colleagues to develop themselves in these attributes and so bring increased learning payoff to the work of the group. The work of the group is, of course, slower and the product of the group may be less impressive than when groups play to strengths. When the group processes (rather than the overall product of the group work) contribute substantially to assessment, a group may choose to play to weaknesses, so that the processes are higher on its agenda and better evidenced in its record of work.

12

Getting groups started

Once group work has gathered momentum, it is likely to be successful. The greatest challenge is sometimes to get that momentum going. The first few minutes can be crucial, and you will need all of your facilitation skills to minimize the risk of groups drifting aimlessly in these minutes. Take your pick from the following suggestions about getting group work going right from the start of a task.

1   **Foster ownership of the task.** Wherever possible, try to arrange that the members of the whole group have thought of the issues to be addressed by small-group work. When possible, allow members to choose which group task they wish to engage in. When people have chosen to do a task, they are more likely to attempt it wholeheartedly.

2   **Start with a short group icebreaker.** Before getting groups under way with the main task, it can be useful to give them a short 'fun' icebreaker so that each group's members get to know each other, relax and become confident enough to work with each other. See the next section for some ideas about icebreakers.

3   **Keep the beginning of the task short and simple.** To Einstein is attributed, 'Everything should be made as simple as possible, but no simpler'. Make sure that the first stage of each group task is something that does not cause argument and does not take any time to interpret. Once a group is under way, it is possible to make tasks much more challenging.

4   **Don't rely only on oral briefings.** Oral briefings are useful as they can add the emphasis of tone of voice, facial expression and body language. However, when only oral briefings are given for group learning tasks, it is often found that after a few minutes, different groups are attempting quite different things.

5   **Use printed briefings.** It is useful to put the overall briefing up on an overhead transparency or PowerPoint slide, but if groups move away into different syndicate rooms they can lose sight (and mind) of the exact briefing. It is worth having slips of paper containing exactly the same words as in the original briefing, which groups can take away with them.

6   **Visit the groups in turn.** It can make a big difference to progress if you spend a couple of minutes just listening to what is happening in a group, then chipping in gently with one or two useful suggestions before moving on. During such visits, you can also remind groups of the deadline for the next report back stage.

7   **Clarify the task when asked.** Sometimes, groups will ask you whether you mean one thing or another by the words in the briefing. It is often productive if you are able to reply, 'Either of these would be an interesting way of interpreting the task; you choose which interpretation you would prefer to address'. This legitimizes the group's discovery of ambiguity, and can increase the efforts they put into working out their chosen interpretation.

8   **Have an early, brief report back from groups on the first stage of their task.** This can help to set expectations that everyone will be required to be ready for later report back stages at the times scheduled in the task briefing. Any group which finds itself unprepared for the initial report back is likely to try to make sure that this position does not repeat itself.

9   **Break down extended tasks into manageable elements.** Often, if the whole task is presented to groups as a single briefing, group members will get bogged down by the most difficult part of the overall task. This element might turn out to be much more straightforward if they had already done the earlier parts of the whole task.

10   **Try to control the amount of time that groups spend on successive stages of each task.** It can be useful to introduce a sense of closure of each stage in turn, by getting groups to write down decisions or conclusions before moving on to the next stage in the overall task.

13

Icebreakers: some ideas

There are countless descriptions of icebreaking activities in books and articles on training; see particularly the books by Jaques and Brandes in 'Further Reading'. An icebreaker is most needed when members of a group don't already know each other, and when the group is going to be together for some hours or days. Most icebreakers have the main purpose of helping individuals get to know each other a little better. Here are some ideas to set you thinking about what the most appropriate icebreakers could be for your own groups. Some icebreakers can be very quick, acting as a curtain raiser for the next activity. Others can be extended into larger-scale activities at the start of a major group project. Don't try to rush these.

1   **Triumphs, traumas and trivia.** Ask everyone to think of one recent triumph in any area of their lives (which they are willing to share), and then ask them to think of a trauma (problem, disaster, and so on) and something trivial – anything that may be interesting or funny. Then ask everyone in turn to share a sentence or so about each. Be aware that this activity often brings out a lot of deep feelings, so keep this for groups whose members need to know each other well or already do so.

2   **What's on top?** This can be a quick way of finding out where the members of a group are starting from. Ask everyone to prepare a short statement (one sentence) about what is, for them, the most important thing on their mind at the time. This helps people to clear the ground, perhaps if they are (for example) worrying about a sick child or a driving test, and enables them then to park such issues on one side before getting down to the real tasks to follow.

3   **What's your name?** Ask everyone in turn to say their (preferred) name, why they were called this name and what they feel about it. This not only helps group members to learn each other's names, but also lets them learn a little about each other's backgrounds, views, and so on. Bear in mind that some people don't actually like their names much, so make aliases acceptable.

4 **Pack your suitcase.** Ask individuals to list 10 items that they would metaphorically pack into a suitcase if they were in a disaster scenario. Emphasize that these items wouldn't have to literally fit into a suitcase and could include pets, but shouldn't include people. Ask them to mill around the room, finding a couple of others who share at least two items from their list. This enables them to get into groups of three or four, with plenty to talk about, before you get them started on the actual group work.

5 **What I like and what I hate.** Ask everyone to identify something that they really like and something they really loathe. Ask them then to introduce themselves to the rest of the group by naming each thing. This helps people to remember each other's names, as well as to break down some of the barriers between them.

6 **What do you really want?** Ask everyone to jot down what they particularly want from the session about to start and to read it out in turn (or stick Post-its on a flipchart and explain them). This can help group members (and facilitators) to find out where a group is starting from.

7 **What do you already know about the topic?** Ask everyone to jot down, on a Post-it, the single most important thing that they already know about the topic that the group is about to explore. Give them a minute or so each to read out their ideas, or make an exhibition of them on a flipchart. This helps to establish ownership of useful ideas within the group, and can help facilitators to avoid telling people things that they already know.

8 **Draw a face.** Ask everyone to draw on a scrap of paper (or a Post-it) a cartoon 'face' showing how they feel at the time (or about the topic they're going to explore together). You may be surprised at how many 'smiley faces' and alternatives there are that can be drawn.

9 **Provide a picture, with small cartoon figures undertaking a range of activities.** Then ask people to say which activity looks closest to the way they feel at the moment (for example, digging a hole for themselves, sitting at the top of a tree, on the outside looking in, and so on). Use this as a basis for getting to know each other through small-group discussion.

10 **Discover hidden depths.** Ask people in pairs to tell each other, 'one thing not many people know about me', that they are prepared to share with the group. Then ask each person to tell the group about their partner's 'hidden secret', such as ballroom dancing, famous friends, ability to build dry stone walls, or whatever. This is a particularly good exercise when introducing new members to a group who already know each other, or when a new leader joins a well-established group.

11　**Make a junk sculpture.** Give groups of four or five people materials such as newspaper, disposable cups, string, sellotape, plastic straws, and so on. Ask them to design and produce either the highest possible tower or a bridge between two chairs that would carry a toy car, or some other form of visible output. Ask them to think, while on task, about the group processes involved (who led, who actually did the work, who had little to contribute, and so on). Then ask them to unpack these thoughts and share in plenary their summarized conclusions about the group processes.

12　**Develop verbal skills.** Ask learners in pairs to sit back to back. Give one of each pair a simple line drawing comprising squares, triangles, rectangles and circles. Without letting their partner see the original, ask those holding the drawings to describe what is on the page, using verbal instructions only, so that their partners can draw the original on a fresh sheet of paper. After a fixed time, let them compare the originals with the copies, and ask them to discuss what the task showed them about verbal communication. A similar task can also be designed by using plastic construction bricks.

13　**Make a tableau.** Ask groups of about seven or eight learners to decide on a theme for their tableau (for example, the homecoming, the machine age, playtime), and ask them to compose a tableau using themselves as key elements. Ask each group in turn to 'present their tableau' to other groups, and then to discuss how they went about the task. Polaroid or digital photos of the tableaux can add to the fun, but do not use this activity if you feel that group members are likely to be sensitive about being touched by others.

14　**Organize a treasure hunt.** Give each group a map of the training centre or campus and a set of tasks to complete across the location. For example, task elements can include collecting information from a display area, checking out a reference item via the Internet, collecting prices for specific items from the catering outlet, drawing a room plan of a difficult to locate study area, and so on. Different groups should undertake the tasks in a different order, so that individual locations (and people) are not mobbed by hosts arriving at the same time. Give a time limit for the treasure hunt and award prizes for all who complete on time. This activity helps people to get to know each other and their learning environment at the same time.

15　**Which of these are 'you'?** Give everyone a handout sheet containing (say) 20 statements about the topic to be explored. Ask each participant to pick out the three that are most applicable to them. Then ask everyone in turn to disclose their top choice, asking the rest to show whether they too were among their own choices.

16   **Interview your neighbour.** Ask participants in pairs to interview each other for (say) three minutes, making notes of key points that they may wish to report back in summary of the interview. Then do a round asking everyone to introduce their neighbour to the rest of the group.

14

Establishing ground rules for groups

Ground rules can be very useful indeed in group work contexts. The following suggestions include some of the issues and starting points from which groups can be encouraged to agree their own set of ground rules.

1 **Create ownership of the ground rules.** The various ground rules agendas suggested below should only be regarded as starting points for each group to adopt or adapt and prioritize. It is important that groups feel able to include ground rules which are appropriate for the particular people making up the group.

2 **Foster a culture of honesty.** Successful group work relies on truthfulness. Suggest that it is as dishonest for group members to 'put up with' something they don't agree about, or can't live with, as it is to speak untruthfully. However, it is worth reminding learners about the need to temper honesty with tact.

3 **Remind group members that they don't have to like people to work with them.** In group work, as in professional life, people work with the team they are in, and matters of personal conflict need to be managed so they don't get in the way of the progress of the group as a whole.

4 **Affirm collective responsibility.** Once issues have been aired, and group decisions have been made as fully as possible, the convention of collective responsibility needs to be applied for successful group processes. This leads towards everyone living with group decisions and refraining from articulating their own personal reservations outside the group.

5 **Highlight the importance of developing and practising listening skills.** Every voice deserves to be heard, even if people don't initially agree with the point of view being expressed.

6 **Spotlight the need for full participation.** Group work relies on multiple perspectives. Encourage group members not to hold back from putting forward their view. Group members also need to be encouraged to value the opinions of others as well as their own.

7 **Everyone needs to take a fair share of the group work.** This does not mean that everyone has to do the same thing. It is best when the members of the group have agreed how the tasks will be allocated amongst themselves. Group members also need to be prepared to contribute by building on the ideas of others and validating each other's experience.

8 **Working to strengths can benefit groups.** The work of a group can be achieved efficiently when tasks are allocated according to the experience and expertise of each member of the group.

9 **Groups should not always work to strengths, however!** Activities in groups can be developmental in purpose, so task allocation may be an ideal opportunity to allow group members to build on areas of weakness or inexperience.

10 **Help group members to see the importance of keeping good records.** There needs to be an output to look back upon. This can take the form of planning notes, minutes or other kinds of evidence of the progress of the work of the group. Rotate the responsibility for summing up the position of the group regarding the tasks in hand and recording this.

11 **Group deadlines are sacrosanct.** The principle, 'You can let yourself down, but it's not OK to let the group down' underpins successful group work.

12 **Cultivate philanthropy.** Group work sometimes requires people to make personal needs and wishes subordinate to the goal of the group. This is all the more valuable when other group members recognize that this is happening.

13 **Help people to value creativity and off-the-wall ideas.** Don't allow these to be quelled out of a desire to keep the group on task, and strike a fair balance between progress and creativity.

14 **Enable systematic working patterns.** Establishing a regular programme of meetings, task report backs and task allocation is likely to lead to effective and productive group performance.

15   **Cultivate the idea of ground rules as a continuing agenda.** It can be productive to review and renegotiate the ground rules from time to time, creating new ones as solutions to unanticipated problems that might have arisen. It is important, however, not to forget or abandon those ground rules that proved useful in practice, but which were not consciously applied.

15

Reducing the bystander effect

Sociologists describe the tendency not to intervene in the crises of others as the 'bystander effect'. The term refers to our hesitancy to help strangers in an emergency, believing that 'someone else' will do something or that we are not suitably qualified to offer the right kind of help. This 'diffusion of responsibility' in a group setting is something that is likely to occur unless we take positive steps to generate involvement.

1   **Make friends quickly.** The bystander effect is prevalent among strangers, not friends or family. One of the ways to overcome it is to ensure that people working together in a group become friends rather than strangers as early in the process as possible.

2   **Create a skills portfolio.** People are more willing to help if they feel they are competent to do so. Share skills and knowledge in the group so that everyone feels they can contribute to each other and the group as a whole.

3   **Actively invite contributions.** The key facilitator or chair can deliberately withdraw and encourage others to come up with answers or ideas. The more often people can help, the more confident they will be about offering help.

4   **Promote small groups or learning circles.** Try to break a large group into fours or fives, where the sense of being a stranger is reduced and people are more likely to offer and take help. The smaller groups can reconvene as a large group with representatives from the small group synthesizing the discussion for the whole.

5   **Extend people's understanding of the nature of 'help'.** People can help by asking questions, by listening, by offering suggestions, by opening their networks and by lending books or articles. Group members should be encouraged to list as many manifestations of 'help' as possible.

6   **Encourage individual accountability.** In a meeting where someone needs help, everyone should feel obligated to assist. The above tips will encourage this behaviour, but eventually people will need to feel accountable for their action or lack of it. The group can discuss this point and produce ideas for generating individual accountability.

7   **Encourage group accountability.** Organizational groups are not composed of individuals who operate in isolation. Most people in an organization are dependent upon each other. The group can be encouraged to identify areas of common ground and see more clearly where everyone overlaps. This will minimize any sense of 'my' and 'your' business.

8   **Create a positive sense of crisis.** An inert state will continue until acted upon differently, to paraphrase Newton. Facilitators can encourage group members to see others' difficulties as not something that will simply be taken care of, but as something which is creating a real problem and will get worse unless someone intervenes.

9   **Identify ownership.** People need to put names and dates against offers of help. Encourage people to go beyond the lame, 'Call me if you need help', to a more specific offer of assistance: a time for the telephone call to take place, a date for a meeting, a name of someone who can give support, and so on.

10   **Review often.** Encourage people to reflect on how they have been acting as individuals and how their behaviour has or has not contributed to other people's learning.

16

Creating group cohesion

Following on from the previous section, the 'bystander effect', where people ignore the plight of others, is a phenomenon to do with strangers. People tend to help people they know, particularly their friends and family. To engender an atmosphere of creative collaboration, it becomes necessary to break down personal barriers and create a sense of unity. The following tips will give you some insight as to how.

1   **Agree that group unity is a good idea.** Personal relations don't work when they're forced on someone. Individuals should be willing to share information about themselves or they will resent any attempts to become more personal. The group can decide if it would be easier, or at least more pleasant, to work among friends, or if some people want to maintain an arm's length relationship.

2   **Decide if arm's length is acceptable.** Some people may not desire a more personal working and learning relationship with others, which is, of course, their right. But, it's also the right of other people to say if they want to include the member in the group. If the group as a whole wants to work closely together, then it may be counterproductive to maintain a relationship with a 'passenger'.

3   **Review why it is important to develop group cohesion.** Remember, there is no such thing as a good group or a bad group – there are only those that more effectively reach their goals. Most researchers agree that collaboration and cooperation are critical success factors of team and group performance. That means the tendency to back away from strangers needs to be supplanted with a more friendly and approachable style.

4   **Encourage group members to agree to get to know one another.** We are more helpful with people we know, which may be a function of birth (family) or friends or neighbourhoods. What we want to do in a learning group setting is to accelerate the process of getting to know each other. We want to mimic the way that people learn about each other in order to deepen familiarity and create intimacy.

5   **Ask them how this happens.** Closeness can't be imposed on people. The facilitator can ask people what it is about others that makes them interesting, and list the items on a flipchart. What questions might we ask to get inside someone's personality and character? The responses will vary from the demographic (age), geographic (birthplace and residence since) to the prosaic – astrological sign, favourite foods, fears, funniest moments, hobbies, and so on. Remember, however, that some individuals strongly value privacy in personal matters.

6   **Let people ask each other.** Preferably in small groups, people can ask each other questions based on the list. Typically, people find the experience enjoyable and revealing, as much about themselves as each other. The small groups can synthesize their findings for the large group, and introduce each group's member in a more relaxed and inviting way than the usual 'introduce the person beside you' format.

7   **Create groups based on friendship.** People may prefer to group according to their original small groups described in the previous point   or they might want to group according to the information they've discovered – foods, star signs, birth orders, hobbies or favourite movies. These shared interests or characteristics may be more meaningful to people than job descriptions or seniority.

8   **Make time for fun.** All the laudable work of the learning group is not necessarily achieved through sheer hard effort. Much of the success of any relationship arises from the fun and spontaneity that people engage in. This kind of fun enriches relationships and can help to smooth the way for every other interaction.

9   **Stay with the moment.** Too much time in groups is spent abstracting a situation out of context. If someone has an idea, a question or needs help, the group should be encouraged to respond to that as it arises. People learn to trust others when their needs are met, not when others talk about them in theory.

10   **Celebrate success and failure.** Anyone can celebrate success, but often it's from making a mistake or failing to meet other people's expectations that we learn something valuable. Being able to share both the good luck and the bad luck stories with others helps us to trust them and feel close.

11   **Encourage group members to recognize appropriate boundaries.** Sometimes people can mistake good working relationships for personal relationships, and on occasion, overstep the mark. It is important that personal space is not invaded literally or metaphorically.

17

Setting shared goals

Any group initiative presumes a common reason, or goal, for the group's existence. This meta-goal may not be exactly the same as individual goals, but they should not be in conflict. How we go about setting goals will be determined partly by the dynamics of the group itself, but the following tips can offer general guidance. The following list of questions can be a useful starting point for a group setting out on a learning pathway.

1   **What is the purpose of the group?** Why have a group at all? People join a group because it is better than working alone. That doesn't mean it is better all the time; indeed, certain activities may best be performed alone and then shared with a group. Writing a first draft, for example, is best performed alone. A group is helpful for sharing the completed first draft.

2   **What is the membership?** Can anyone join your group? Can they come and go? What about missing a meeting? The nature and behaviour of group members should be discussed at the first meeting.

3   **How do you want the group to be?** What are the desired group norms? Ask each other what kind of behaviour is expected, what it will look like and what the consequences are for not exhibiting it. For example, 'mutual respect' may be a goal, but what does it look like? Not interrupting each other or agreeing to offer constructive criticism may be 'respectful activities' that become group norms.

4   **What is likely to stop the group from reaching the goal?** Each individual comes with his or her own personal history, likes, dislikes, fears and hopes. Forming a group doesn't cause those personal differences to vaporize! Groups should discuss and remain aware of individual differences and predilections, some of which may be counter to group processes and activities.

5   **What about leadership?** Will the group's goals be managed by the group or will responsibility mostly be vested with one person? Leaders may come and go depending on the group's need or function, or the group may decide to appoint a leader. In the interest of collaborative learning, the leadership roles should be discussed and reviewed frequently.

6   **Who has what power?** Some people in the group may be perceived as more powerful due to, for example, position in the organization or their specialist knowledge. How will people's power help or hinder the group to achieve its purpose? Part of the group's statement of behaviour or norms should articulate the issue of how power is to be shared.

7   **How will goals be met?** Goals can be broken into shorter-term tasks with responsibility taken by individuals or by smaller subsets of the larger group. People can self-monitor progress, but should be encouraged to share progress with everyone else to truly facilitate group learning.

8   **What will be the life cycle of the group?** A group grows in maturity just as individuals do. People should share their views and experience of the group's growth from the initial, exciting moments of 'birth' through the awkward middle period where frustrations may arise. The changing dynamics can be observed and the group encouraged to discuss and recommit.

9   **What will the group do when it has achieved its goals?** Both the tasks and the processes can be tracked so that people know how the group is working and how its goals are being attained or not. And what happens when you 'get there'? Many groups decide to continue to work together well beyond the initial period when a task or a goal has been accomplished. This kind of group will decide that the process of learning together is a sufficient goal, although the process may be best served by again creating tasks or projects.

10   **How will the group end?** If the group is at an end point, evaluation of the process is usually helpful, both to create learning points for the future and also to give a feeling of completion. People should be able to define 'what worked and why' as well as 'what didn't work and why'.

Chapter 3 Particular group learning contexts

This chapter aims to provide some food for thought about the different rationales for particular learning contexts for groups. A key factor is whether or not a facilitator or tutor is present during the group work. We start with 'tutorials' – the most common group learning scenario in higher education, but also the least valued one as shown by feedback from learners. The suggestions here aim to turn tutorials into learning experiences that are valued much more highly. Next, we look at working with groups of mature students on distance learning programmes. This is a special case of the general discussion of tutorials, but it is important to take due account of the different expectations that such learners have.

Then, we look at 'home groups', 'action learning sets' and 'tutorless groups'. These have much in common, but can be used to best effect when the rationale and intended learning outcomes are clearly understood, both by group members themselves and learning facilitators.

Finally, the chapter ends with two sets of suggestions about being involved in group contexts yourself, whether as a teacher, trainer or facilitator of learning.

18

Tutorials

Tutorials, seminars and other small-group situations can be highly productive learning experiences for learners. Larger overall class sizes make it more difficult to provide such occasions for learners and it is, therefore, important that the quality of those sessions that are provided is as high as we can make it. The following suggestions may help you to enhance the quality of learners' learning in small groups.

1   **Make sure that the goals of each tutorial are clearly communicated to learners.** Sometimes the goals can be published in advance, while on other occasions they will depend on the questions and issues that the learners bring to the occasion. In either case, the learning payoff is enhanced if the goals are established or reviewed at the start of the session concerned.

2   **Help learners to know the purposes of small-group work.** Learners often don't really know what the differences are between the different kinds of teaching–learning sessions on their timetables, in terms of the different sorts of behaviour expected of them, and the teaching–learning processes involved in each kind of small-group work. The more learners know about why you are giving them each different episode of small-group work, the better they can benefit from such occasions.

3   **Prepare for small-group sessions!** There is a tendency (as noticed by teaching quality reviewers!) for tutors to prepare well for lectures but not for tutorials. This leads learners to come to their own unfortunate conclusions about the relative importance of each of these teaching–learning environments.

4   **Start each new group session with a short icebreaker.** This helps each group's members to get to know each other, relax and become confident to work with each other. There are dozens of icebreakers that take no more than five minutes to run. Experiment with them and find your own favourites, then invent better ones.

5 **Keep the beginning of the main task short and simple.** Make sure that the first stage of each group task is something that does not cause argument and does not take much time to interpret. Once a group is under way, it is possible to make tasks much more challenging.

6 **Don't talk too much!** A problem with small-group sessions is that it is all too easy for the tutor to fill all of the available time. Even when answering learners' questions, it is usually more productive to provide good short answers to several questions than an in-depth definitive answer to just one question.

7 **Make good use of question and answer processes.** Come in to a small-group session with a list of questions you may or may not actually ask, and concentrate first on all the questions you can draw from the learners. Towards the end of a tutorial, you can select from your 'unanswered' questions some for the learners to prepare their own answers to be ready for a future session. It can be useful to give each member of the group a different question to go away with (but make sure that none of the questions are so difficult that the learners will not return on the next occasion).

8 **Ensure that learner participation is high on the agenda.** Getting all the learners to participate is quite an art. Just asking for verbal contributions can allow the confident, pushy learner to dominate. Asking each of the learners to write down their own immediate answers to a question, for example, on Post-its or small pieces of overhead film, can be a way of promoting equal participation opportunity and can help the more retiring learners to provide their contributions to the group. Vary the nature of learners' activities, for example, getting them to make flipchart lists, Post-it replies to questions, mind-maps, pictorial metaphors, flowcharts, and so on.

9 **Think about introducing learner managed small-group sessions.** These can be occasions where the learners themselves are given freedom to prepare the content and then manage the processes by which they tackle the topic concerned.

10 **Don't ask questions that just depend on recall.** It is much more useful to consider questions that help learners to make sense of what they are learning, than just to remind them about what they may have forgotten.

11 **Don't ask too many questions at once.** Learning in small groups happens best when the learners know exactly which question or issue they are addressing at a given time. It can, however, be useful to write up the 'whole' list of questions on a flipchart or whiteboard so that learners can see where each question fits into the whole picture.

12 **Don't put a learner on the spot with a difficult question too early!** This can deter learners from participation, and can even make them so uncomfortable that they may choose not to attend your next session. It is much more acceptable to put some of the learners on the spot with hard questions towards the end of the session, but moving away from them if they have not got ready answers, as these questions can then be the agenda for the next session so giving all the learners involved some time to prepare their answers.

13 **Don't ask questions, then answer them yourself.** Although it can be hard to wait for learners to work towards the answer to a question, and you may be itching to provide the answer, learners will learn a lot more by struggling if necessary. You can help them to converge towards a good answer by giving feedback on those parts of their thinking that are along the lines required, and explaining to them why other ideas are not correct or appropriate.

14 **Don't ignore learners' answers.** Even when learners give incorrect or confused answers to a question you've asked them, they need some helpful feedback on their answers and not just to be told what the right answers should have been. Where possible, build on learners' own responses when leading towards the correct answers.

19

Tutorials for adult distance learners

Group tutorials, when it is feasible to arrange such provision, can play a major part in the learning experience of mature students on distance learning programmes. The following suggestions may assist you to help them to get the most from group tutorials.

1 **Don't lecture to them!** While it can be tempting to fill up the available time trying to teach important parts of the syllabus, it is better to get distance learners to interact with each other as much as possible. This encourages them to continue to use each other as a resource between group meetings.

2 **Don't cancel meetings at short notice.** Distance learners often travel considerable distances to attend group tutorials, and are very put out if they arrive only to find that a meeting has had to be cancelled or rearranged.

3 **Get to know their names.** If you only see distance learners from time to time, it can be harder to learn their names than is the case with students you meet more regularly. Use name cards, badges or sticky labels so that you get to know their names more quickly and to help them to get to know each other.

4 **Work out some intended learning outcomes for each tutorial.** Show these on an overhead or slide, or give them as a handout, so that learners can remember them better than if you were just to announce the overall aims of the session.

5 **Don't plan too many intended learning outcomes!** It is better to plan in detail only enough to fill half of the time available, so that you can give plenty of time to matters arising that learners themselves will bring to the tutorial.

6   **Encourage distance learners to contact you with their agendas for group tutorials.** For example, give them a cut-off date by which to e-mail you with questions they would like you to go over in each tutorial. Ask them to let you know in advance which parts of their learning materials they are finding most difficult.

7   **Use tutorials to go through matters arising from work you have already assessed.** It can be useful for distance learners to take comfort from the fact that many of them may have experienced the same problems with assignments. When you are sure which distance learners are likely to be attending face-to-face sessions regularly, you can then reserve some of the detail of feedback on their work for tutorials. Conversely, make sure that learners who don't or can't attend tutorials get enough written feedback, so they are not unduly disadvantaged by missing the tutorials.

8   **Help distance learners to develop appropriate study skills.** This can be an ongoing agenda at tutorials. Mature students often appreciate help with such matters as essay writing technique, revision strategies and exam technique. Giving due attention to study skills in tutorials also has a significant positive effect on students' attendance patterns.

9   **Use group tutorials to give distance learners some experience of informal peer-assessment.** For example, get all of the students in a tutorial to assess an example of a past essay or assignment, then help them to see how useful it is to make judgements on someone else's work as a means of deepening their learning of the subject matter covered. When the atmosphere is right, you can then lead them into peer-assessing some of each other's work, perhaps draft assignments, which will later be marked formally by you.

10   **Be willing to extend the tutorials informally.** Distance learners often benefit from continuing to talk to each other after a tutorial, for example, in a convenient pub or lounge area, and may welcome the opportunity to take their tutor along, too.

20

Home groups

Home groups are often used in colleges and universities where an ethos of group learning is being fostered intentionally and strategically. 'Home groups' is the term used to describe a relatively long-term group which stays together through thick and thin along a diverse learning pathway. Home groups come together all the way along a learning pathway, so that members can exchange experiences and learn from each other's triumphs and disasters alike. The following suggestions may help you to help learners get the most from being members of home groups.

1   **Give home groups time for members to get to know each other.** Home groups are often intended to be safe, non-threatening environments, where group members can share their moans as well as their successes. It is important that members of home groups develop trust in each other, so that they relax and get the most from each other's support and help.

2   **Give home groups something interesting to do to start them off.** It is not really important that this icebreaking task is relevant to the future work of the group. It is more important that it brings group members together well. It is therefore particularly important that the first home group task is not threatening, and not assessed in any way.

3   **Decide carefully how you wish to constitute home groups.** Revisit the suggestions elsewhere in this book about forming groups, and decide whether you want to leave home group membership entirely to learners themselves or to constitute the groups yourself strategically. Both extremes have their own advantages and drawbacks.

4   **Make sure that home groups are quite distinct from other group constitutions.** For example, it is important that a home group is quite different from an action learning set or syndicate allocated a particular learning objective. The major strength of a successful home group can be the disparity of its members' experiences.

5   **Cause home groups to get together quite regularly.** It is worth giving home groups tasks, from time to time, that will then be followed up by members either individually or in completely different group settings. They then come to regard their time in home groups as feeding in substantially to the central parts of their learning.

6   **Think about your own level of facilitation in home groups.** You may wish to play a significant role in early meetings, to set the tone of the group and to underline its importance. However, it can be really useful to back off once the groups are working well, and to give the groups the comfort of privacy in which to share and exchange members' experiences, problems and triumphs.

7   **Legitimatize home groups as the place where members can be themselves.** For example, when other parts of their learning are proving difficult, home groups should be seen as a place where worries can be shared and peer-support can take place quite informally.

8   **Set questions from other group contexts to be taken back to home groups.** It is important that home group time is seen by members as being well spent in the overall pattern of their learning, and that key questions and issues central to the learning programme are aired and debated in home groups.

9   **Set preparation for other group contexts to be done in home groups.** This helps to establish the place of home groups in the bigger picture. When home groups are working well, it leads to a lot of relevant preparation being achieved before other group settings, making them more productive and efficient.

10   **Make sure that home groups finish well.** Ideally, a good home group will want to (and may find ways to) continue after the official lifetime of the group. The group should not fizzle out when the learning programme is over. It is much better if the group is allowed to come to a resounding and memorable conclusion in one way or another.

21

Action learning sets

Action learning sets can have some things in common with home groups, not least effective peer-support and confidence building processes. The difference is usually that action learning sets have relatively prescribed learning outcomes, and the overall work of the sets is likely to be subject to some kind of formal assessment. The following suggestions may help to trigger your own ideas about how best to use action learning sets in your own contexts.

1   **Don't make action learning sets too big.** As with any other learning group, there is likely to be an optimum size dependent on the nature of the tasks the group is intended to engage in. Four members is often a suitable minimum constitution, and six members may be a sensible maximum to avoid the likelihood of passengers or bystander behaviours.

2   **Think carefully how the membership should be established.** An action learning set that has chosen its own membership is likely to have strengths regarding identity, but when free choice is used as the overall strategy, there are bound to be 'remainder' groupings, which set off to a much less happy start.

3   **Action learning is about achieving learning objectives.** Sometimes, these may usefully be prescribed by the facilitator or tutor. When possible, however, it is better to allow action learning sets some freedom in their interpretation of the intended objectives.

4   **Action learning is about learning from experience.** This is just as much about learning from things that went wrong as from things where no problems were encountered. Help group members to value the business of 'what we learnt about ourselves from this' both for positive learning experiences and more traumatic ones.

5   **Consider setting the objectives, but allowing the group to determine the evidence they will furnish for their achievement.** This allows the curriculum covered by action learning sets to be reasonably closely defined, while still allowing the groups some freedom in their interpretation of how they will demonstrate that they have reached the specified targets.

6   **Suggest that the leadership of action learning sets is rotated appropriately.** This can mean different members taking the lead for different tasks and contributing to the overall work of the set.

7   **Consider allowing action learning sets to negotiate their own learning outcomes.** Where particular standards are required to be evidenced, some care will need to be taken to assist action learning sets to strike a sensible balance between overambitious outcomes and underachievement.

8   **Consider the scope for renegotiation of outcomes and evidence of achievement.** When action learning sets have some freedom to adjust their targets, timescales and products, the increased ownership of the agenda that they develop manifests itself in better group learning.

9   **Help action learning sets to track their own work.** For example, suggest that records are kept, such as the agendas for their meetings, the decisions they reached, the areas where consensus was achieved straightaway and the issues that caused disagreement. These records, suitably prepared, can lend themselves to assessment of the work of the group, whether self-assessment by the group members themselves or tutor assessment.

10   **Legitimatize 'any other business'.** Action learning sets should not just feel that they have to stick rigidly to their agreed or negotiated intended outcomes. Other useful learning that occurred on the way to their achievements can be every bit as important as the intended learning. Allow scope for sets to keep records of their own 'unexpected' learning as well as their intended learning.

22

Tutorless groups

Tutorless groups overlap with home groups and action learning sets, both of which can function in a tutorless mode for at least some of their working lifetimes. It can also be useful to establish tutorless groups for particular purposes, which are different from those of action learning sets or home groups. The following suggestions may help you to think of how you may relinquish control of appropriate parts of group learning for your own learners.

1   **Brief tutorless groups on the purposes of this way of learning.** Ensure that they understand the value of the process and don't just see it as tutor cop-out.

2   **Brief tutorless groups clearly.** Ensure they have clear guidance on the tasks expected of them and the likely outcomes they should be aiming to achieve.

3   **Provide clear backup.** Build in checkpoints at intervals, so tutorless groups don't feel they are struggling alone to make sense of their learning. However, ensure that in checking progress, you don't overdirect in developing group activities.

4   **Prepare for problems.** Let groups know how they can get help if they have genuine problems that they can't solve themselves, but try to make sure that they set out to be as self-reliant as reasonably possible.

5   **Consider using tutorless groups for resource-based learning.** For example, rather than suggest that learners undertake elements of open learning or computer-based learning individually, ask them to do these elements in small, specially constituted groups. The peer-group learning which can occur when a small group works through an open learning resource together is often far reaching.

6　**Consider the most appropriate task size for tutorless groups.** The overall task needs to be big enough to be worthwhile, but not so big as to be crucial if the group fails to gel well. The tasks do need to be important, however, as otherwise learners may regard tutorless groups as a luxury rather than as a key part of their intended learning.

7　**Consider rotating the membership of tutorless groups.** While home groups and action learning sets work best when their membership is constant over a significant time period, tutorless groups can be effective for much shorter tasks with different membership for each task. Such rotating membership can actually add to the feeling of belonging to the other kinds of groups.

8　**Make the most of learners explaining things to each other.** Tutorless groups are particularly appropriate for situations where some learners have already mastered a topic, but need consolidation by explaining it to others.

9　**Give tutorless groups the means to assess their own achievements.** When devolving the learning to people, it is appropriate to devolve the assessment too – at least as far as allowing the groups to assess their own learning in privacy before any formal assessment of it is undertaken.

10　**Suggest that tutorless groups should accumulate evidence of their work.** If, for example, the product of a tutorless group task is to be assessed in due course, the product itself will be evidence of the achievement of the group, but may not lend itself to being evidence of the processes that the group went through, or of the relative contribution to the work of the group by individual members. It can be useful to suggest to groups that they should, in their own way, gather evidence of how they did what they did.

11　**Keep a safe distance from tutorless groups.** Tempting as it may be to test the temperature of the groups to see that they are working effectively, it is better to test the product of their learning in ways that do not interfere with the freedom of the groups to operate in their own way.

12　**Process is important, but should be free from interference from tutors.** While it may be appropriate from time to time for tutors to monitor the group processes that occur in home groups or even action learning sets, in tutorless groups it could undermine the special responsibility that group members can have for making their own processes work well. Testing the products of tutorless groups can, in its own way, be a sufficient incentive to group members to sort out their processes.

13   **Suggest that tutorless groups should rehearse for forthcoming assessments.** In the absence of an authority figure, the group can safely discuss views on likely tasks or exam questions and can work out what needs to be done to prepare for these. When a tutor is present, there is a tendency for learners to wish not to show what they don't yet know.

14   **Gather feedback about the value of tutorless groups.** Ask learners what they found most useful about the process and what they found least useful. Also ask them what they enjoyed most and least, and what they learnt about themselves from the process. Build on their feedback in your future design of tutorless group task briefings and processes.

23

Be a group member yourself!

One of the problems teachers find when starting to facilitate group learning is that they may not often have been participants in group learning themselves. Many lecturers' experiences (at least as they remember them) of learning have been as individuals (even in group settings), rather than as group members. The following suggestions may help you to empathize more with learners, when your intention is for them to learn in group contexts.

1 **Work out the benefits for you.** While it is all too easy for academics to plough lonely furrows in the world of academia, not all success indicators are linked to individual scholarship and achievement. Successful group or team attributes are likely to advance your career, as well as to make your job more interesting and fulfilling overall. Don't let the dark side of collaborative experiences overshadow the benefits of working well with colleagues.

2 **Make the most of group learning in staff development settings.** Staff developers often find academics make quite awkward group members! Abandon, at least temporarily, any tendencies you have to show your individuality and leadership, and allow yourself to be an ordinary member of a group in group exercises in staff development programmes.

3 **Don't be tempted to lead the group.** Academics tend to be leaders, partly because that's what students often expect of them, and partly because of the drives that led them to their chosen careers. Try, at least role-play, being a follower for some of the time in group situations. More followers than leaders are needed at any instant in any effective group.

4 **When you're being a follower, play with what makes good followership.** Also play with what makes bad followership, but not sufficiently to destroy the work of the group. Finding out for yourself about the skills of good followership helps you to be better able to counsel students about how to work well in groups.

5   **Sometimes you will, of course, be a leader in group situations.** Try to watch yourself leading at the same time as exercising leadership. Try to capture the skills that add up to good leadership, so that you can unpack them in your advice to students who are developing their group working skills.

6   **Cultivate patience!** Often in group work, you will have the feeling that you could learn something much faster if only you got on with it on your own. This may well be true. However, depth of learning does not always go with speed of learning and group learning can indeed be deeper.

7   **Try to find something useful to learn entirely in group contexts.** Look for something you don't need to learn, but which will be interesting in its own right and useful in some way to the rest of your life. Then use it as an agenda to explore long-term group learning processes and study how group dynamics unfold and develop. Also explore the factors which can destabilize long-term groups.

8   **Step back and watch yourself in group contexts in your everyday life.** Think about academic groups and social groups, too. Become more alert to the things you carry away from such group contexts, and reflect on which kinds of learning seem to be associated with particular types of group behaviour and structure.

9   **Engage in committee watching!** Committee meetings are likely to be group experiences that you may feel you get too much of! It can relieve the frustrations somewhat to use some of the time you spend in the less productive meetings to observe group behaviours. Look out for those behaviours that lead to effective group work and those that hinder it.

10 **Try a Belbin analysis.** There are various techniques that help to unpack group and team roles, and the Belbin approach can shed some light on the role or roles you adopt most naturally in group situations. For the analysis to give you most data, you need to find other people who can report objectively on how they see you as a team player, to compare and contrast with your own self-perceptions about your approaches and attitudes. If you find the analysis particularly useful, you may wish to extend it to those of your students who have important group or team elements in their studies, or who need to develop their group behaviour awareness to prepare for their career destinations.

24

Team teaching

One of the most productive ways to develop your own techniques for working with groups of learners is to work as a member of a group yourself in the course of your normal teaching. Below are listed some of the benefits for you in engaging in team teaching, as well as some suggestions about how to get the most from the processes involved.

1   **Plan very carefully for team teaching.** Don't just expect things to fall into place naturally, even (or particularly) if the colleagues with whom you are co-working are people you know very well.

2   **Talk through how you will share out the 'air time'.** Plan the session so that you both (or all) are clear about who is leading and who is supporting at any point in the session.

3   **Discuss in advance the extent to which everyone is comfortable with improvisation.** It can be very disconcerting to the rest of the team if one member goes off at a tangent, but it can also lead to some very interesting sessions.

4   **When observing, resist the temptation to jump in uninvited.** In team teaching, you may often be expected to join in freely when someone else is leading, but take care not to do so just because you think you see a better way of doing what they are doing. Allow colleagues to run group sessions their way and learn from that.

5   **Make the most of having someone else there with you.** It can be really useful to allow your colleague to chip in when you run out of steam now and then. If you're finding something particularly hard to explain to your learners, it is often the case that someone else can put it another way and help them to understand it.

6   **Be receptive to feedback from colleagues.** Teaching is often a relatively private activity between teachers and learners, and can feel somewhat intimidating when there are other colleagues present as well. If you're defensive when colleagues make suggestions and observations about your work, the flow of useful feedback to you will be stemmed.

7   **Regard peer feedback as useful preparation for teaching quality review.** When you are accustomed to having other tutors in your group sessions, it is much less threatening to have an observer present in more formal circumstances.

8   **Learn from your colleagues' approaches.** When you are present in other people's group sessions, you can always be alerted to useful tips and wrinkles. Notice things that work well and emulate them in your own way in your own sessions. Notice also things that don't work well and find your own ways of avoiding them in your group work.

9   **Use team teaching to increase your awareness of group processes.** Working with colleagues can be a high-level group activity. Don't forget to step back from the curriculum content from time to time and think about what is happening in the group. Remind yourself of the range of feelings (positive and negative, constructive and destructive), which can accompany any kind of collaborative activity. Use what you learn to help students to work together more effectively in group situations.

10 **Make notes for yourself.** Whether observing a colleague working, or being observed yourself, it is useful to find a few minutes to jot down your own notes of matters arising to use as an *aide-mémoire* later. One's best thoughts tend to evaporate quite quickly if not captured in a few written words at the time.

11 **Become better able to substitute for colleagues when necessary.** It's always useful to be able to do a colleague a favour and, with experience gained from team teaching, your colleagues are much more able to make a substitution for you on those occasions where you really need someone to cover for you.

Chapter 4   Exercises and processes for groups

What you *do* with your groups will depend on all sorts of factors, including:

- the nature of the subject matter they are studying;

- the sizes of the groups;

- the ways the groups were formed in the first place;

- whether or not the group work is being assessed in some way;

- the facilities available;

- the nature of the learning environment in which the groups are working;

- the overall timescale of the group work.

In this chapter some ideas are presented about particular group exercises and processes. The aim is to encourage you to work out appropriate ways to develop effective and interesting group processes in your own subject area and with your own learners.

The chapter ends with some detail of a particular group exercise used by the author in the context of a training programme about risk assessment from chemical hazards. That topic used to be regarded as 'boring', but the group exercise described in the case study attracts much warmer reactions from learners.

25

Ringing the changes

There are many different ways of enhancing the quality of learning in learning groups. The following suggestions expand on the question and answer ideas for use in tutorial type sessions given earlier in this book, and are among the processes that teaching quality reviewers are looking for in their observations of group work.

1   **Get individual learners to prepare and present seminars.** This can include the learner leading the seminar by taking questions from the rest of the group, and perhaps also from the tutor involved in the group. The attention of the learner audience can be significantly increased by getting the learners receiving the seminar to use processes of peer-assessment with straightforward and well expressed criteria, which have preferably been formulated by the learner group.

2   **Consider getting pairs or groups of learners to prepare and present seminars.** This can be less intimidating than solo performances and can involve the development of useful cooperation and collaboration skills. Peer-assessment can help all the learners involved to get more from such seminars.

3   **Use tutorless groups for appropriate learning activities.** These give learners the freedom to contribute without the fear of being found lacking or making mistakes in front of a tutor. For such groups to work well, it is useful to provide the learners with carefully formulated briefings in print and to require an appropriate report back product.

4   **Use buzz groups in large group sessions.** These are particularly useful for generating in an informal way a lot of ideas or opinions, which can then be reported back and explored in greater depth with the large group. Even in tiered lecture theatres, it is quite possible to have episodes of buzz group activity, where people discuss, argue or debate ideas with those closest to them in the theatre.

5   **Use brainstorming techniques to generate ideas.** This is useful in small groups and still works well with groups of 20 or more learners. It is important to formulate strict ground rules for brainstorming, such as 'give no comment on ideas already given', 'say "pass" if you've nothing to add when it's your turn', and 'think creatively and say anything that comes to mind'. After producing as many ideas as possible in a few minutes, the group can start prioritizing and clustering them.

6   **Use snowballing or pyramiding to refine ideas.** This can be a way of enhancing learning in quite large groups by getting learners to work together in a structured way. For example, get learners to think of ideas in pairs, then combine with another pair to take the ideas further, and then combine with another four to prepare a report back to the whole class.

7   **Use crossovers to enhance learners' communication in groups.** For example, divide a group of 16 into four groups of four. Set the small groups a first-stage task, then ask one member from each group to move to another group and report the findings. Set the second stage of the task to the revised groups, then ask a different member to move on and report. Continue doing this until everyone has worked with everyone else.

8   **Consider using fishbowls in medium-sized groups.** For example, from a group of 20 learners, six could be drawn (or volunteer) to sit in a circle in the middle of the room. The inner circle could then be briefed to discuss a scenario, with everyone else observing, and with an exchange mechanism by which learners from outside of the group wanting to make contributions could replace someone in the group.

9   **Use role play to help learners to contribute more easily.** Some learners, who are reluctant to contribute to group discussions or debates because of shyness, lose most of such inhibition if they are playing someone else. Printed handout sheets giving sufficient details of each role to help learners to adopt the role they are intended to play, and are useful for allowing each learner to react to the other roles involved as they unfold in the role play.

10 **Self-help groups can enhance learners' learning.** It can be worthwhile to start such groups up with tutor support, and help the learners in each group to start out to generate their own ground rules and targets. Then the groups can be left to operate without further support, other than perhaps a mechanism to bring unresolved problems to a class meeting or to a tutor.

26

Post-it exercise on how people learn

The following sequence of activities can be very useful for alerting people to the principal processes underpinning effective learning. It helps them to have ownership of these processes and to make use of them consciously in their learning. These Post-it reminder note exercises are based on some of the thoughts about learning processes outlined in Chapter 1 of this book.

1   **Issue four Post-its to everyone and brief them as follows.** 'I'll be asking you four questions about your own learning. Each question is in two parts. Just think about the first part, then write your answer to the second part on a Post-it. Just write a few words for this, in large letters, so it can be read easily when placed on view.' If you can, use Post-its of four different colours. This can help the resulting exhibition to be more attractive and can draw out the trends more successfully.

2   **How do you learn well?** 'Think of something you do well – something you're good at. It could be academic, professional, or a hobby or sport. Write on a Post-it a few words about how you came to do this successfully.'

3   **Make exhibition one.** Ask people to stick their Post-its on a flipchart (or wall, or door). Let them see for themselves the most common factors. Expect to draw out from these: practice, learning by doing, learning through trial and error.

4   **What makes you feel good?** 'Think of something you like about yourself – something that gives you a sense of pride. Write a few words on the next Post-it about why you feel good about this – what's your evidence? What's the basis of this positive feeling?'

5   **Make exhibition two.** Allow the group to see for themselves the most common factors, which are very likely to revolve around feedback, other people's comments or reactions, praise and seeing tangible results.

6   **What stops you learning?** 'Think of something you're not good at. Write a few words on the next Post-it about what went wrong in learning this, and who (if anyone) was to blame.'

7   **Make exhibition three.** All sorts of factors are likely to come up in this, but draw out examples of 'didn't want to learn it in the first place', 'breakdown in communication', 'didn't understand it', and 'poor teaching'.

8   **What keeps your learning going?** 'Think of something you're good at, but didn't want to learn at the time. Write down on your final Post-it a few words about what kept you at it.'

9   **Make exhibition four.** Many different factors are likely to arise here, but expect to be able to find motivators like 'needed it for what I wanted to do next', 'strong positive support from someone', 'didn't want to let someone down'.

10   **Sum up the five main factors underpinning successful learning.** From the combined Post-it collections, you should be able to draw out overriding confirmation for the following five factors:

   * learning by doing – including practice, repetition and learning from mistakes;
   * learning from feedback – other people's reactions;
   * wanting to learn – intrinsic motivation;
   * needing to learn – extrinsic motivation;
   * making sense of what has been learnt, 'digesting' it, increasing understanding of it.

27

Feedback exercise for groups

To help people make the most of their opportunities to learn from each other in groups, it can be useful to give groups an exercise on the following lines to help them to think about the process of giving and receiving positive and critical feedback from each other.

1   **Ask the overall group to work in pairs.** If there is an odd number in the room, suggest that a trio is formed as well. When (as is often the case in larger groups), you feel that they haven't yet decided who is going to work with whom, give the further direction to, 'Hold up the hand of the person you're going to work with', which quickly helps them to decide!

2   **Ask everyone to think of a compliment about the person they're about to work with.** Point out that it doesn't matter if they've only just met, or if they've known each other for years. Watch (but don't comment on) the likely behaviour which results – mirth!

3   **Now ask everyone to say the compliment to their partner.** Usually there will be a considerable amount of laughter.

4   **Help the group to analyse what has just happened.** Ask, 'Why did you laugh?' The usual replies are along the lines of 'embarrassment', 'felt uncomfortable', and so on. Point out that laughter, in the nicest possible way, amounts to not taking the compliment on board and, indeed, rejecting the words of the person giving the compliment.

5   **Suggest that next time a compliment is exchanged, it is acknowledged and received.** Suggest that words such as, 'Thank you for that' or, 'I'm glad you like that' are used, both to help the compliment to be properly received and to reduce or remove any embarrassment.

6   **Consider commenting on the cultural factors influencing how people receive positive feedback.** It is only in some cultures (not least the British one) where people tend to shrug off positive feedback. Suggest that this kind of false modesty is in fact a barrier to using feedback to enhance learning.

7   **Now ask everyone to think of a small element of critical feedback about their partner.** Decide whether you're going to go through with the remaining steps outlined below, or just to let your learners think about the implications of these steps. You'll know whether your learners are up to these steps.

8   **Ask people to exchange critical comments.** Then ask them to think what happened during the process. Did their eyes narrow and go 'cold'? Did they feel their defence mechanisms coming into play?

9   **Suggest that next time some critical feedback is received they thank the person providing it.** Words such as, 'Thank you for telling me about this' or, 'It is useful for me to know this, thanks' can make the person offering the critical feedback much more willing to do so again when it is needed, as well as indicating that the critical feedback has been duly taken on board by the person who has received it.

10 **Summarize why you have given the group these exercises.** If they are aware of their instinctive reactions both to positive and critical feedback, they will be better able to step back from such instincts and to analyse and use both kinds of feedback as they learn from each other in future.

28

Post-its and flipcharts

Getting things down on paper is often a vital element in keeping group learning going. The largest common size of paper is the A1 flipchart and the smallest the Post-it (which come in various sizes, of course). The following suggestions may help you to decide which medium to use for which purposes.

1   **Use Post-its for private brainstorming.** When all members of the group are intended to think in parallel, before putting together their ideas, it is useful to give everyone one or more Post-its on which they can write their individual ideas or questions.

2   **Use Post-its to overcome 'blank sheet fright'.** Faced with a whole sheet of paper on which to jot down ideas, people often become inhibited and don't know quite where to start. A Post-it is much smaller and less challenging, and helps people to make that first step, getting at least one idea down in words.

3   **Use Post-its for individually named contributions.** Getting everyone in a group to write their names on each Post-it, along with their contribution, allows ownership of ideas to be kept track of. This can, however, inhibit free brainstorming of ideas, so it is important to use names only when there is a good reason for doing so.

4   **Use Post-its as an equal opportunity medium.** One of the problems with oral brainstorming is that it can so easily become dominated by the most extrovert or confident members of the group. Writing ideas on Post-its overcomes the inhibitions of the less forthcoming members of the group.

5   **Use Post-its to save time transcribing ideas to a flipchart.** It can be painfully slow for a facilitator or group scribe to write up all the ideas onto a flipchart. It is much faster to simply stick the Post-its onto a flipchart to present a visual display of all of the ideas generated. Also, transcription tends to be unfaithful, and people's meanings often become distorted by the words chosen by the transcriber, causing a loss in the sense of ownership individuals have regarding their ideas.

6   **Use Post-its for prioritization.** When everyone in a group has written some ideas onto Post-its, it is much easier for the whole group to attempt to prioritize the ideas in order of importance (or practicability, or likely payoff, and so on). This can be done by rearranging and readjusting the Post-it display on a flipchart, with the most crucial ideas at the top and the less important ones further down. It can be very productive to get groups to choose and prioritize only the top nine ideas by using a 'diamond-9' formation on the flipchart.

7   **Use Post-its for public readings.** For example, ask everyone to write down their personal answer to a question (or view on an issue) in summary form on a Post-it anonymously. Then ask people to swap their Post-its around until they no longer know who has theirs. Ask everyone in turn to read out what is on the Post-it they now have. You can then reply to each person's contribution, knowing that you are not going to offend them if you say something critical about the contribution as it was not their view

8   **Use flipcharts to create something that can be shown to other groups.** A display of Post-its adhered to a flipchart is fine for the group that created the ideas, but is less suitable for sharing with other groups because of the size of handwriting. It is worth summarizing the ideas, which may have been generated on Post-its, onto a freshly drawn flipchart, using marker pens and colour to emphasize importance and links between ideas.

9   **Use flipcharts to exchange between groups.** A very productive way of exchanging ideas between groups, without tedious repetitive report back stages, is for one member to cross over to another group bearing the flipchart product from the previous group, and to talk the new group through the thinking behind the flipchart. It is then useful to get the new groups to add further ideas to the flipcharts by asking them to extend the original task in specified directions.

10   **Use flipcharts for exhibitions.** This is especially useful when different groups have been tackling different issues relating to an overall theme. Pasting the flipcharts to a wall and allowing all group members to circulate round them can be more interesting than listening to a series of report backs from each group. This can be further enhanced when one member of the group that created each flipchart, stands by the exhibit to explain it as necessary to visitors.

11   **Details on flipcharts can be captured and circulated.** This is, of course, possible when electronic flipcharts are available and allows a printout of the contents of a 'chart' to be made and copied to all members of the group. However, it is becoming more attractive to have a digital camera and to snap each chart, then loading the contents into a computer and printing them out with editing or explanations added, if necessary. Once such equipment is available, the running costs are almost negligible.

29

Helping learners to write reflections on group learning

Many learners who work in groups or teams are asked to write a reflective piece on the way in which their group worked. Learners are asked to reflect on what happened, and particularly their own role within it, in order to consolidate what they have learnt and to draw out lessons for the future. However, this activity can present a number of problems, and you need to give some guidance on how to write in this way and how the writing will be assessed.

1 **Start with description.** Good reflection should be based on a clear account of who did what, when, what kinds of difficulties were encountered, and so on. Reflection without description is usually far too vague, impressionistic and sloppy.

2 **Use a framework for analysis.** After the description, you will be expecting learners to analyse group activities. You could provide a framework for this or help learners to develop one. One possibility is a set of prompt questions such as: What was the group trying to achieve at this point? What were the different views? What was said and what was left unsaid? How was the decision made? How did you feel about this? How did other group members feel? What were the group energy levels and motivation like at this point? Did anything unexpected happen?

3 **Lead into action planning.** A key purpose of individual reflection is to gain a better understanding of what happened in group work and your personal role within it. Ask learners to identify what they contributed to the group and what difficulties they experienced, and then to use this to identify their own strengths, weaknesses and issues they would like to address in future.

4   **Encourage the linking of theory and experience.** Most learners who are asked to work in groups have been introduced to some relevant theories about working collaboratively. Encourage them to draw on such theories and to discuss how they might apply these to their own experiences in relation to motivation, leadership, team roles, competitiveness, and so on.

5   **Develop ground rules for writing about other group members (and the tutor).** All kinds of problems can arise if group members write about other learners or the tutor in ways that are inappropriate. Some learners may be reluctant to write anything about their peers if they know that the tutor will see it. Some ground rules might be: don't make assumptions about the motives and feelings of other learners - check by asking them or, if this is not possible, acknowledge that it is only your perception, for example, 'Stuart seemed to me to be upset'. Don't write anything about a fellow learner that you would not want them to read (even if you don't expect them to read it). Such rules may seem unduly restrictive, but in many professional contexts we need to be able to comment on and criticize the behaviour of others in a constructive way and learners need to learn how to do this.

6   **Ask learners to focus on critical incidents.** Where learners have participated in a lengthy group task, their written reflections will, of necessity, be selective. Ask them to identify two or three 'critical incidents' that were turning points for the group, or that illustrate particular difficulties or successes, and concentrate on those.

7   **Help learners to learn how to write reflectively.** Ask them to write a short piece on a small element of group working; for example, about the first one-hour meeting of the group, on how the group divided tasks up or how the group responded to feedback from the tutor. Give feedback on these early attempts. Encourage learners to share what they have written within the group, so that they can see the different approaches and learn from each other. Show learners examples of good pieces of writing that would score highly on your assessment criteria.

8   **Make the assessment requirements clear.** Learners are often very unsure about what kinds of things it is acceptable to write in a reflective piece. Is it OK to admit to having made mistakes? Is it OK to talk about how you felt? Would it be OK to say that you stayed up until 3.00 am to write your section of the group report on the day before it was due to be handed in? Clear indications that you are looking for elements such as clear descriptions of what went on in the group, analysis of successes and difficulties, and acknowledgement of feelings and concerns will help learners to decide what to write.

9   **Decide whether you really want to assess reflective writing!** There are many problems with assessing it, so perhaps you don't need to! The most useful purpose for reflective writing is for individual learners to learn from their reflections and also acquire the habit of reflecting on experiences and learning from them. (Reflective writing is not actually a very good way of telling you, as a tutor, what 'really' went on in the group!) If you need to assess something, perhaps it could be a list of action points or strengths and weaknesses, supported by selected extracts from the learners' reflections on the group.

10   **Make reflection a group activity.** Rather than individuals writing a reflective commentary, the group could discuss what went on, what they achieved, what problems were encountered, and so on. They could then agree a written group statement covering the aspects required for assessment.

30

Virtual group work

Using computers is often thought of as a solitary activity. Computers can, however, be very useful for group activities. Group working can have many advantages, ranging from the interchange of ideas to providing social contact. Working together at a distance may sound paradoxical, but sometimes it is easier to arrange group activities in this way. Because of computer communications, some barriers of distance and timing can be removed. In order for your learners to participate, they will need e-mail facilities as a bare minimum.

1   **Think carefully about the number of people who should be in each group.** If groups are too small, the learners may have to work too hard and they may not have all the skills needed for the task. If the groups are too large, they may be unwieldy and it might be difficult and time consuming for decisions to be made. In large groups, there is a risk that skills can be duplicated so that some people are underutilized.

2   **Decide whether you will choose who is in which group or whether the learners will organize themselves.** If you choose, you have more control over the whole process of group working. If the learners organize themselves, they will feel more empowered and will be taking more responsibility for their work.

3   **Think about the task the groups will have to tackle and how it affects the composition of the 'ideal' group.** Some tasks require special skills and it may be necessary to distribute skill holders among the groups. These skills could be related to the task in hand, or they could be group skills such as leadership.

4   **Develop group tasks that enable individuals to use their particular skills.** Your learners may not all have learnt the same skills or some may be more proficient in some areas than others. Carefully chosen group tasks can involve real team work in distributing tasks among the group, so that people can use their skills effectively.

5   **Use group tasks to help to distribute skills.** Someone who is particularly proficient in a skill can help other members of a group to improve their skills. This has an additional benefit of making the skilled person think hard about what they can do in order to show another person how to do it.

6   **Encourage computer communications between learners as soon as possible.** In order to make effective use of computer communications, regular use is needed. If learners can develop a culture of frequently checking e-mail and conferences, they will make very effective use of these media. If they only check occasionally, there will be a struggle to establish their effective use.

7   **Set some simple tasks early on.** You could pair learners up and give them a simple task that requires them to exchange ideas. They could then produce a joint word-processed report on what they have done. This would mean that they would need to communicate with each other, and they may also need to exchange files attached to e-mail messages.

8   **Give everyone some practice at using computer-conferencing.** If you plan to use computer-conferencing to keep learner group work going after a face-to-face course, or between elements of such a course, it is useful to use part of the course time to get everyone talking to each other electronically. Ideally, you will need a room with networked terminals for each learner. It can be useful to start everyone off with a common interest topic, even one that has no relationship to your teaching programme, and allow your learners to concentrate on the process of communicating with each other electronically, rather than thinking too hard about the content of their practice communications.

9   **Put out some important information only by e-mail or in conferences to make people check for it.** Rather than sending out all the documents by mail, or as issued handouts, use computer communications for some of it. Warn your learners that you are going to do this and keep doing it so that they continue to check their e-mail and conferences.

10   **Make sure some kind of backup is available.** If someone didn't receive a computer message because of technical problems, it could cause major problems for them. Some sort of safety net could be used; for example, you could send out a message to all learners every week. Anybody who didn't receive the message would know to contact you so that you could try again or send a paper copy to them in the normal mail.

11 **Decide on your own access to group conferences.** The groups' conferences could be closed to you, so that you cannot read them and learners can discuss any topic freely. This may help learners to feel uninhibited about what they say in messages. Alternatively, you could have access to them so that you can monitor progress. Make sure that the learners know what you have decided so that they can behave appropriately!

12 **Make use of any facilities the conference software has for tracking who has done what.** Most packages have features that show who has contributed, read or revised different items of a conference. These enable some checking over who has done what they were supposed to.

13 **Make sure that somebody is in charge of the group.** It is easy for a group to encounter serious problems if there is no control over its activities. One person needs to take on the role of coordinating the whole group to make sure that all the tasks are progressing properly. When groups undertake several successive tasks, encourage the groups to decide who will coordinate their work on a rotating basis.

31

A case study

Suggested activity

Before looking at this case study, think of a particular group task that you use in your own work with learners. Jot down your own answers to the following questions:

- What works best with this as it stands?
- What are the main problems with this group task?

Next, as you read through the case study, think about whether it sparks off ideas of processes that you could weave into your own group task, to make it work even better.

'Questions to ask the boss'

This is an exercise developed by the author for use in training workshops on chemical hazards. Typically, there are between 15 and 25 participants present, and the exercise is used near the start of a one-day session on chemical hazards during a one-week course on Occupational Health. The process of risk assessment is quite complex, and the exercise is designed to get people into the process even if they have not done anything like it before. The exercise is divided into a series of separate tasks as described below. To give the feel of the case study, the task briefings are reported below exactly as they would be said (or displayed on-screen) during the workshop session. Many of the processes (particularly the 'diamond-9' one) lend themselves to all sorts of alternative group activities. So, as you read this case study, make notes to yourself about how you could adapt the processes to your own curriculum.

Task 1

Suppose your boss has told you you're going into a room and will be working there with a hazardous chemical substance. Your boss says, 'OK, any questions?' Jot down privately half a dozen or more short, sharp questions you might ask the boss. You've got two minutes.

Task 2

Now working with three other people, compare and contrast the questions you've all come up with. Write what you agree are the most important of these down on Post-its, one per Post-it. Five minutes. (I give each team a small pile of Post-its – a different colour for each team.)

Task 3

Now, in your fours, prioritize your Post-its by shuffling them around on the table until you've got the top nine into a 'diamond-9' order with the most important question at position 1, and so on.

	1	
2		3
4	5	6
7		8
	9	

Task 4

Next, I want each team to bring out their 'number 1' most important question, and stick it onto the flipchart, which has four boxes on it, and place your question in the most appropriate box as follows:

- Hazards: eg What is it? Is there a data sheet? Is it toxic? Has a risk assessment been done?, and so on.

- Precautions: Protective clothing? Exhaust ventilation? Breathing apparatus? Emergency?, and so on.

- Exposure: How long? How often? How much of the substance?, and so on.

- Other: Why me? What training will I have? Why use this substance?, and so on.

Hazards:	Other:
Precautions:	Exposure:

Task 5
'Free-for-all': now bring all your other Post-its and place them in the most relevant box.

Feedback from learners on the exercise

They *don't* find it at all boring! They find it fun. This is because they're *doing* things. They're doing a variety of things. In particular, they like the 'diamond-9' part of the exercise, because this leads to vigorous debate among the teams. They also like the multicoloured final display that they build up on the flipchart – it's *their* prioritization and classification of risks, not mine. I don't actually mention to them the variety of things they're doing, because they don't need to be aware of the processes, but they are roughly as follows:

Task 1: brainstorming, in the comfort of privacy.
Task 2: discussing, sharing, deciding.
Task 3: prioritizing.
Task 4: sorting out what sort of question the most important one is.
Task 5: completing the picture, further decision making, comparing their views with other people's.

After they've completed the whole exercise, I point out that they've just done a quite ambitious, if general, risk assessment exercise starting from scratch. We continue to use the flipchart with their questions on it as a reference agenda for many further exercises and discussions for the rest of the training day.

History!

How did I come up with this exercise? By getting it wrong at first – in other words, more boring! I used to ask them for questions, which I then wrote down on the flipchart. That took time, and it was my writing, not theirs – and sometimes my words, not theirs. It was also then my classification, not theirs. And it took longer – more boredom. When they do it as outlined above, the whole thing takes less than 30 minutes, and as soon as it's done we take a coffee break (usually with a hubbub of productive chatter about the exercise continuing).

Chapter 5   Groups behaving badly?

When things go wrong, sometimes it's the fault of the group members themselves. Sometimes the blame can be directed at the facilitator. Sometimes the institutional context can be the source of the problems. In this chapter, we look in turn at some of the most common 'damaging behaviours' and offer for each a few suggestions which can alleviate the problems that can result from them. The chapter ends with some suggestions on how to approach two of the most common overall problems in group learning: conflict and gender issues.

32

Group member behaviours that damage group work

The following section looks at a range of learner behaviours that can damage or even destroy group work. These are based on the experience of many facilitators. For each of these behaviours, some tactics are offered below as to how facilitators can reduce the effects on group work.

Group members being late

Sometimes lateness is unavoidable, but even then it is seen as time-wasting for the group members who have managed to be punctual. Here are some approaches, from which facilitators can select, to reduce the problem.

1   **Lead the group towards including an appropriate ground rule on punctuality.** If the group members feel a sense of ownership of such a ground rule, they are more likely to honour it.

2   **Point out that punctuality is related to courtesy.** Remind group members that when one of them is late, it is an act of discourtesy to all the other people who have been kept waiting, including the group facilitator if present.

3   **Lead by example – don't be late yourself!** If the facilitator is late, it is not surprising that group members can fall into bad habits. Your own actions are seen as a reflection of how you value group learning.

4   **Make the beginning of group sessions well worth being there for.** If group members realize that they are likely to miss something quite important in the early minutes of a group session, they are likely to try harder to be punctual.

5   **Give out something useful at the start of the session.** For example, issue a handout setting the scene for the session, or return marked assignments straightaway as the session starts.

6   **Avoid queuing.** If the place where a group meeting is due to be held is frequently still occupied at the starting time for the group session, it can be worth rescheduling the group for five or 10 minutes later, so that a prompt, punctual start can be made then, without those who arrive early having to hang around.

Group members not turning up at all

This is one of the most common complaints made by facilitators. Learner non-attendance can have a serious effect on group work, and a variety of approaches (and incentives) can be used to address the problem, including those listed below.

1   **Ensure that it really is worth turning up.** If group members are not getting a lot out of group sessions, they naturally value them less and this can lead to them being lower priority than they could have been.

2   **Keep records of attendance.** Simply making notes of who's there and who's not gives the message that you're really expecting learners to turn up and join in. If keeping records isn't enough, see below.

3   **Assess attendance.** For example, state that 10 per cent of the coursework element of a programme of study will be based solely on attendance. This is one way of making quite dramatic improvements in attendance at small-group sessions. However, the downside of this way of inducing learners to attend is that some group members may be there in body but not in spirit and can undermine the success of the group work.

4   **Issue something during each session.** Learners don't like to miss handouts, task briefings or the return of assessed work. It is important to make missed paperwork available to learners who could not have avoided missing a session, but don't be too ready to do so for those who have no real reason for absence.

5   **Cover some syllabus elements only in small-group sessions.** When learners know that these elements will be assessed alongside those covered in lectures, and so on, their willingness to attend the small-group sessions increases.

6   **Don't cancel small-group sessions.** Learners are quick to pick up the message that something that has been cancelled could not have been too important in the first place. This attitude then spreads to other people's small-group sessions.

Group members not preparing

Group members can get far more out of small-group sessions if they have done at least some preparation for them. However, many teachers and facilitators complain that learners still arrive without having thought in advance about what the session will be covering. It is difficult to make every group member come prepared, and overzealous attempts to do this are likely to cause unprepared learners to decide not to come at all. The following suggestions may help you to strike a workable balance between getting well-prepared learners, and frightening them off.

1   **Help learners to structure their preparation.** For example, issuing an interactive handout for them to complete and bring to the forthcoming session is better than just asking them to, 'Read Chapter 3 of Smith and Jones'. Instead, you could ask them to 'research your own answers to the following seven questions using Chapter 3', and leave spaces beneath each question for them to make notes as they read.

2   **Don't fail to build on their preparations.** If group members go to the trouble of preparing for a session and then nothing is done with the work they have done, they are discouraged from preparing for the next session.

3   **Try starting each session with a quick quiz.** Ask everyone one or two short, specific questions, and perhaps ask respondents themselves to nominate the recipient of your next question. This is a way of building on the preparation work that learners have done, and making sure that everyone is included, rather than just those who are most forthcoming when you ask questions.

4   **Consider asking them to hand in their preparations sometimes.** This does not necessarily mean that you have to assess them, but you could sift through them while group members are busy with an activity to gather a quick impression of who is taking preparation seriously. The fact that you did this occasionally would lead to learners not wishing to be found lacking, should it happen again, and lead to better levels of preparation.

5   **Get them to peer-assess their preparations sometimes.** This has the advantage that they can find out how their own learning is going compared to other learners. It also helps them to learn from feedback from each other, and the act of giving a fellow learner feedback is just as useful as receiving feedback.

Chatting inappropriately

Small-group sessions are indeed occasions when you want learners to talk to each other and to learn by explaining things to each other. The dangers of inappropriate chatter can be reduced; the following suggestions may spark off your own ideas about how best to attempt this.

1   **Don't assume all chatter is actually inappropriate.** Quite often, if you explore further why some group members are chatting, you will unearth good reasons, such as someone explaining something to someone who doesn't yet understand it or helping someone who missed something to catch up.

2   **Go closer to the people who are chatting.** If the chatter was indeed inappropriate, they will usually stop. If it was something of value, you may wish to join in and help.

Departing early

Relatively few learners risk the embarrassment of leaving formal learning situations, such as lectures, before the end. With small-group work, there is a tendency for premature departure, or for learners to drop out at a natural break in the session and fail to return for the continuation of the session. The following suggestions may help to minimize such behaviours.

1   **Keep groups busy.** One of the most common causes of learners slipping away early from group sessions is that they think there is nothing important still to do. It may be better to give groups too much to do in a given time slot rather than too little, as long as you also ensure that there is time for 'unfinished business' in future meetings.

2   **Be careful with breaks.** If your session is long enough to warrant a refreshment or comfort break, negotiate a firm restart time. Write this on a flipchart, overhead slide or markerboard, so that everyone sees it as well as hears it. It can be more memorable to use 'odd' reconvening times, such as, '10.43 please' rather than, 'Quarter to 11 please'.

3   **Make the last stages of group sessions particularly valuable to learners.**
    For example, help learners to summarize what they've been doing. Make
    debriefings as important as briefings. Sometimes, give out a really useful
    handout right at the end.

Not doing their jobs

A lot of time can be wasted when group members go off on tangents to their
intended tasks or procrastinate about starting the next stage of their work.
Work avoidance is human nature – at least for some of the time for some people!
The following approaches may help you to keep your group members on task.

1   **Have clear task briefings in the first place.** It is usually better to have
    these in print and for every learner to have a copy. Oral briefings are
    quickly forgotten and are much more likely to lead to deviation from the
    intended tasks

2   **Make the first part of a group task relatively short and straightforward.**
    This can cause a group to gain momentum more quickly, and this can
    help to ensure that later, more complex tasks are started without undue
    procrastination.

3   **Specify the learning outcomes clearly.** When learners know what they
    should be getting out of a particular activity, their engagement is enhanced.

4   **Set structured tasks with staged deadlines.** Most effort is expended as
    the deadline approaches, especially if learners will be seen to have slipped
    if their task is not completed by a deadline. Act as timekeeper if you are
    facilitating group work: gentle reminders such as, 'Six minutes to go,
    please' can cause a lot of work to be done.

Being disruptive

Group work is often damaged by one or more participant whose behaviour
slows down or diverts the work of others. Disruption is more of a problem in
small-group contexts than in formal lectures as it takes less courage to be
disruptive in informal settings. Sometimes, there is no easy solution for
disruptive behaviour, but the following suggestions may help you to solve
some such occurrences.

1 **Check that it really is disruption.** If you're a passing spectator to different groups, you may happen to arrive at one particular group just at the moment when one of its members is expressing a strong feeling or arguing a point relatively forcefully. This may be fine with the other members of the group, and it gives the wrong message if the facilitator assumes the worst.

2 **Find out why a person is being disruptive.** Sometimes there are identifiable reasons for such behaviour, for example, when a group as a whole has become dysfunctional, or when the task briefing is being interpreted in different ways by group members.

3 **Watch for the same group member being disruptive repeatedly.** It is then usually worth talking to the person concerned, to find out why this may be happening. If this does not improve the situation, it may be necessary to reconstitute the membership of groups for successive tasks, so that the disruptive element is fairly distributed across a wider range of learners, rather than a particular group becoming disadvantaged by recurring disruption.

Dominators

These can be among the most serious enemies of effective group learning. They need to be handled with considerable sensitivity, as their 'taking over' the work of a group may be well intentioned.

1 **Get the group to reflect on how it is functioning.** For example, once in a while, give them a relatively small task to do as a group, even an exercise that is primarily for light relief. Then when they have completed it, ask them to think through their answers to questions, such as the following:

- How well do you think you did that as a group?
- Did someone take the lead, and if so, how did this come about?
- Who said most?
- Whose ideas are most strongly present in the solution to the task?
- Did you always agree with the ideas being adopted by the group?
- Was there anything you thought but didn't actually say?

This can cause the group to reflect on any elements of domination which may have occurred, and can reduce the tendency for domination in future group activities.

2   **Lead a discussion on the benefits and drawbacks of assertiveness.** Then ask group members to put into practice what they have learnt about assertiveness. This can lead to learners watching out for each other's assertive behaviours, and reduce the chance of a particular group member dominating for too long.

3   **Confront the dominator privately.** For example, have a quiet word in a break or before the next group session. Explain that while you are pleased that the dominant group member has a lot to contribute, you would like other learners to have more opportunity to think for themselves.

4   **Intervene in the work of the group.** Sometimes it is helpful to argue politely with a person who seems to be dominating, to alert other group members to the fact that they could be being led off target by this person. Be careful, however, not to put down the dominator too much – there's little worse for group dynamics than a sullen exdominator!

Not listening to other group members' contributions

This can undermine the productivity and ethos of groups of all kinds, from student group work to high-powered committees. There is no simple solution to the problem, but you can choose which of the following tactics could at least help with the problem.

1   **Address the issue in a general briefing.** For example, present the saying: 'We all know how to try to help someone who is hard of hearing, but it's much harder to help someone who is hard of listening'.

2   **Use an exercise.** For example, include a group task where at some stage everyone is asked to jot down or report back on the gist of what each other group member said about an issue. This can sometimes alert non-listeners to their problem.

3   **Include an element of peer-assessment of contribution.** Clarify that listening well to others' views counts as an important element of contribution. When group members know that their contribution (including effective listening) is to be evaluated at some stage, they are likely to try (perhaps subconsciously) to make sure that they are aware of their own contribution to the group.

Know-all behaviour

This can lead to an extreme form of dominating behaviour. Some of the tactics suggested for domination continue to apply, but you might wish (or need) to go a little further. Consider these additional possibilities.

1   **Let the group sort this out for themselves.** Sooner or later, most groups will turn on a know-all – usually at the first suitable occasion when the know-all is proved to be wrong! However, the group dynamics can be seriously damaged if things go this far, and the know-all may not recover from the setback and undermine further work of the group.

2   **Have a quiet word with the know-all.** Point out, perhaps, that such behaviour can be interpreted as not just over-assertive, but also quite aggressive by others. Sometimes it is enough that you have noticed the behaviour, and the person concerned will move quite comfortably into a less aggressive stance in the group.

3   **Don't reward the know-all.** Even when this person is right, be careful to give them credit, but give the credit to the group as a whole. This can help to remind a know-all that it is the product of the group you are interested in, not that of individual members.

33

Group facilitator behaviours that can damage group work

There are many ways in which group learning facilitators can damage group work. Sometimes facilitators know about the things they do that undermine the success of group work, but more often they are simply not aware that things could be improved. When facilitators know they have a bad habit, it would be tempting to simply advise, 'Stop doing it!', but often this could lead to the reply, 'Yes, but how?' The following list of facilitator 'faults' is rather longer than the learners' damaging behaviours already discussed, but it can be argued that facilitators are able to address their own shortcomings even more directly than they can help learners to address theirs. As before, each situation is annotated with some suggested tactics for eliminating or reducing the various kinds of damage that can occur.

Ignoring non-participants

It is tempting to ignore non-participants, hoping either that they will find their own way towards active participation or that other group members will coax them out of inactivity. Alternatively, facilitators sometimes take the understandable view that, 'If they don't join in, they won't get as much out of the group work, and that's really up to them to decide'. However, there are indeed some straightforward steps from which facilitators may select to make positive interventions to address the problem of non-participation as and when they see it.

1   **Remind the whole group of the benefits of equal participation.** This is less embarrassing to the non-participants themselves and can be sufficient to spur them into a greater degree of involvement.

2   **Clarify the group learning briefing.** Place greater emphasis on the processes to be engaged in by the group and less on the product that the group as a whole is to deliver.

3   **Consider making the assessment of contribution to the work of the group more explicit.** When non-participants know that participation counts, they are more likely to join in.

4   **Confront a non-participant directly.** This is best done tactfully, of course. The simple fact that it was noticed that participation was not enough is often enough to ensure that the situation does not arise again.

5   **Try to find out if there is a good reason for non-participation.** There often is. Sometimes, for example, a non-participant may find it difficult to work with one or more particular people in a group situation because of pre-existing disagreements between them. It may then be necessary to consider reconstituting the groups or see whether a little 'group therapy' will sort out the problem.

6   **Explore whether non-participation could be a cry for help.** The act of not joining in the work of a group can be a manifestation of something that is going badly for non-participants, possibly in an entirely different area of their learning or their lives in general.

7   **Check, with care, whether the problem is with the work rather than the group.** Non-participation can sometimes arise because of the nature of the task, rather than being anything to do with the composition or behaviour of the group. For example, if the group learning task involves something to do with researching the consumption of alcoholic beverages, it is not impossible that someone whose religion forbids alcohol resorts to non-participation.

8   **Check whether non-participation could be a reaction against the facilitator.** If someone does not like the way that you are organizing some group learning, their reaction could be not to join in.

Allowing domineerers

Domination has already been discussed under the bad habits that group members can engage in, and several tactics have already been suggested there. However, if you allow domination, it can be seen as your fault, too. The following tactics may include remedies for situations where you notice group learning being undermined by domineerers.

1   **Have a quiet word with the domineerer.** This is often enough to solve the problem. Having been seen to be too domineering is usually enough to make a domineerer stop and think.

2   **Get the whole group to do a process review.** For example, give them a relatively straightforward collaborative task to do, then ask them all to review who contributed most, why this happened, whether this was fair, and whether this is what they want to happen with the next (more important) group learning task.

3   **Watch out for why people dominate.** Sometimes, it's because they are more confident and it's important not to damage this confidence. It can be better to acknowledge group members' confidence and experience and gently suggest to them that they need to help others to develop the same, by being able to participate fully in the actions of the group.

Lack of preparation

We've already explored some of the tactics that can be used to solve the problem of lack of preparation by group members. This time, the issue is lack of preparation by the facilitator. The short answer is, of course, 'prepare'. However, the results of this preparation need to be visible to group members. The following approaches can help to ensure that group members can see that you are taking group work as seriously as you want them to do.

1   **Make it obvious that you have prepared specially for the group session.** There are many ways of allowing your preparations to be visible, including:

   • Coming armed with a handout relating to the particular occasion, rather than just any old handout.

   • Researching a current topic and presenting the group with material on it.

   • Arriving punctually or early to avoid the impression you were delayed by getting your own act together ready for the session.

   • Making sure that you have indeed done anything you promised to do at the last meeting of the group.

2   **Keep records of group sessions and have them with you.** You would not arrive to give a lecture or presentation without having your notes and resources with you, and doing the same for group sessions gives the message that you take such sessions just as seriously as larger-scale parts of your work.

Being too didactic or controlling

This is one of the most significant of the facilitator behaviours that can damage group learning, and experienced facilitators can be the most vulnerable! The quality of group learning is greatly enhanced when learners themselves have considerable control of the pace and direction of their own learning. The following suggestions may alert you to any danger you could be in.

1   **Don't try to hurry group learning too much.** It is particularly tempting, when you know very well how to get the group to where it needs to be, to intervene and point out all the short cuts, tips and wrinkles. It is much better, however, for group learners to find their own way to their goals, even when it takes somewhat longer to get there.

2   **Hide your knowledge and wisdom sometimes.** In other words, allow group members to discover things for themselves, so that they have a strong sense of ownership of the result of their actions. As mentioned previously, this may be slower, but leads to better learning. Don't, however, make it show that you are withholding help or advice. When you feel that you may be giving this impression, it is worth declaring your rationale, and explaining that it will be much better for your group learners to think it out for themselves before you bring your own experience to their aid.

3   **Allow group learners to learn from mistakes.** Tempting as it is to try to stop learners from going along every blind alley, the learning payoff from some blind alleys can be high. Help them back from the brick wall at the end of the blind alley, rather than trying to stop them finding out for themselves that there is a brick wall there.

4   **Plan processes rather than outcomes.** It is well worth spending time organizing the ways that group learners can work towards their goals, rather than mapping out in too much detail the things they are likely to experience on the way. The achievement of the group learning outcomes will be much more enduring when the group has ownership of the learning journey towards them.

5   **Ask your learners.** Many of the things that can go wrong in teaching or training could have been avoided if feedback had been sought on the way. The best way of getting feedback is to ask for it, not just to wait for it. To get feedback on important things (such as whether or not you are being too didactic or controlling), there's no faster way than asking for exactly that.

6   **Learn from selected colleagues.** Feedback from other group learning
     facilitators is always useful. However, it is worth going out of your way
     to seek feedback from colleagues who have a particular gift for making
     group learning productive, and being duly selective in the tactics you
     add to your own collection.

Poor interpersonal skills

This is a really difficult one! It is true, nevertheless, that some group learning
situations are damaged by the lack of interpersonal skills of the facilitator. It's
not very helpful to advise, 'Go and improve them!' The following list of
suggestions may help if you suspect that this problem could be yours.

1   **Find out anyway.** If you imagine that interpersonal skills could be getting
     in the way of the success of group learning situations you are involved
     in, ask people about it. The real problem is often far less daunting than
     the imagined one.

2   **Work the extent of the problem out for yourself.** For example, get into
     the habit of taking a tape recorder into your group sessions and playing
     extracts of the recordings back to yourself from time to time. Don't be
     secretive about the tape recorder – you need, technically, to have the
     permission of everyone else present to record their voices. Explain (for
     example) that you are researching the way your groups are functioning
     and emphasize that you're not assessing group members' contributions.
     If you find tape recordings really useful, it could be worth your while to
     go further and have a camcorder in your sessions from time to time. Even
     the most experienced group learning facilitators continue to learn a great
     deal about their interpersonal skills, by seeing themselves in action every
     now and then.

3   **Use group processes that are less dependent on your interpersonal skills.**
     For example, if you're not too comfortable with giving a presentation to a
     group, prepare a handout instead. Allow learners to explore the handout
     for themselves, and then initiate a group discussion of the matters arising.

4   **Remind yourself that good interpersonal skills aren't everything.** You
     could, for example, be a leading expert in a field of study and just not
     happen to be very skilled at helping groups of people to explore it. Don't
     undervalue the strengths that you bring to group learning. Keep looking
     out for ways you can put your strengths to even more use, rather than
     worrying about particular weaknesses.

Lack of cultural sensitivity

This is a serious group damaging behaviour. In fact, lack of cultural sensitivity can be more dangerous in small-group situations than in large-group ones. It is also one of the hardest areas to find out about. Few people are brave enough to challenge a group learning facilitator with this crime! It is useful for even the most skilled group learning facilitators to undertake a regular self-audit on this issue. The following tactics can help.

1   **Read about it.** There is no shortage of published material on equal opportunities, cultural issues, and so on. Sometimes, when reading this literature, one can be surprised by the thought 'but sometimes I do this too!'

2   **Watch other group learning facilitators, with this agenda in mind.** See what they do to avoid the pitfalls and also notice when they fall into them. Work out alternative approaches that could have circumvented such problems.

3   **Don't make assumptions.** It is particularly dangerous to bring to your role of learning facilitator any preconceptions about the different members of your groups, such as those based on gender, age, ethnic group, perceived social status and any other area where assumptions may be unwise and unfounded. Treating people with equal respect is an important part of acknowledging and responding to individual difference.

4   **Talk to group members individually.** When you are working with a mixed group, for example, it is in your informal, individual conversations with members of the group that you are most likely to be alerted to anything that could be offending an individual's cultural or personal perspectives.

5   **Ask directly sometimes.** It is important to pick your times wisely, and to select people who you believe will be willing to be frank with you if necessary. Rather than asking too directly (for example: 'What do I do that could be culturally insensitive?'), it can be useful to lead in more gently, for example: 'What sorts of learning experiences do you find can be damaged by people who are not sensitive enough culturally?', 'How does this happen usually?', and so on.

Favouring clones!

This happens more often than most people imagine. It is noticed straightaway by everyone else in the group! It can go entirely unnoticed by the perpetrator. It is, of course, perfectly human to have 'warmer' or 'more empathetic' feelings and attitudes towards someone who is more like oneself than other people, or who shares significant attitudes, values, and even 'looks'. In particular, teachers of any sort can be flattered and encouraged when they recognize 'a disciple' among a group of people. If you think you could be in danger of indulging in this particular behaviour, think about which of the following approaches may be most helpful to you.

1 **Go clone detecting!** From time to time, think around the types of people who make up the learning groups you work with, and test out whether any of them are more like you are (and particularly more like you *were*) than the others. Then watch out for any signs that you could be treating them differently (even if only slightly).

2 **Don't overcompensate.** It is just as dangerous to be too hard on clones as to favour them. The person concerned may have no idea at all why you are being harder on them rather than on other people. The people you might (consciously or subconsciously) regard as clones may have no inkling that they are in this special position! Subconsciously, you could be putting them under the same sort of pressures as you put yourself under long ago, and exacting of them the standards you applied to yourself.

Talking too much

This is one of the most common of all group learning facilitators' bad habits. However, it is just about the easiest to do something about. The following suggestions should contain all you need to rectify this problem – if you own it.

1 **Remind yourself that most learning happens by doing, rather than listening.** Concentrate on what your group learners themselves do during group sessions, rather than on what you do.

2 **Don't allow yourself to be tempted into filling every silence.** In any group process, short episodes of silence are necessary components – space for thinking. When you happen to be expert enough to step in with your thoughts, before other people have had time to put theirs together, it is all too easy to be the one to break the silence. What seems to you like a long silence, seems much shorter to people who are busily thinking. Let them think, then help them to put their thoughts into words. When they have ownership of putting together ideas and concepts, their learning is much deeper and more enduring.

3 **Only say some of the things you think.** Being the expert in the group (you probably are!), you're likely to know more than anyone else about the topic being addressed. You don't have to reveal all of your knowledge, just some of it. Don't fall into the trap of feeling you have to defend your expertise or that you need to justify your position.

4 **Don't let them let you talk too much!** It's easier for group members to sit and listen to you than to get on with their own thinking. Sometimes, they can encourage you to fill all of the time and opt for an easy life.

5 **Present some of your thoughts (particularly longer ones) in print.** Use handouts to input information to the group, but not at the expense of getting group members to think for themselves. You can convey far more information in five minutes through a handout than you could in five minutes' worth of talking. People can read much faster than you can speak, and in any case, they can read a handout again and again – they can't replay you speaking (unless they're recording it – and even then, would they really replay it all again?).

Intimidating learners

Not surprisingly, this can damage group learning. It does, however, often come as a surprise to group learning facilitators that they can be seen as intimidating. The following suggestions may alert you to some of the circumstances where this can happen, despite your good intentions.

1 **Wear your expertise and wisdom lightly.** You may have more than you think. To people who are new to a subject, your expertise may seem quite formidable.

2   **Be aware of your other roles.** For example, you may be assessing the work of group members now or later. This in its own right can cause a certain degree of intimidation, especially if group members imagine that you're assessing their every word – or that every second of silence, while they're thinking how to respond to one of your questions, is being added up.

Putting learners down

Few group facilitators would deliberately set out to put learners down. Yet, many learners feel that this is exactly what sometimes happens to them in learning groups. The following suggestions may alert you to ways that your group learners could feel put down.

1   **Take care not to 'dump on ideas'.** This is how learners sometimes perceive the actions of facilitators. You may know, from your experience, that a particular idea will not lead the group to a successful outcome, but it is important not to make the person who thought of the idea feel that it is being ridiculed or dismissed lightly.

2   **Watch your language, particularly that concerned with assessment or judgement.** For example, the word 'satisfactory' is hardly ever pleasing to people whose work or ideas are labelled with the word. Nor is 'adequate'. Obviously, 'poor' or 'weak' are negative, damaging words. Such words are sometimes described as 'final language', and there is no way of recovering from the harm that such words can do to learners' feelings and motivation. 'Fair' is almost as bad. 'Excellent' is also final language, but in a much less damaging way. Many of these judgement words are most dangerous when written rather than spoken. For example, you could say 'very satisfactory' in an entirely positive tone, whereas when written, the reader's interpretation could be 'far less than good'.

3   **Remember that your words may be taken more seriously than you expect by learners.** Sometimes, they will react much more acutely to things that you, as a group facilitator, say, than they would have done if the same words were used by fellow group members. Therefore, for example, if you happened to repeat something critical that one of them had said about another's ideas, it would be your words that produced the most damage. You are likely to be regarded as an authority, even if you don't feel yourself to be one.

4   **Don't forget body language.** An exasperated sign, a grimace or a sigh are each a powerful 'putting down' message of one sort or another. Your body language is observed quite acutely by members of your groups. Body language that is positive causes no problems; it is the critical body language that gets noticed.

# Failing to invite equal contributions

Many parts of this book address the issue of facilitating group work in an equitable way. In the context of damaging facilitator behaviours, it is important to remember that learners themselves often write in their feedback notes about failure to have the chance to make equal contributions to group processes. Sometimes, this may indeed have been their own fault, but nevertheless their impression is often that the issue should have been addressed directly by the facilitator. Here are some reminders about a few processes whereby you can try to ensure that no one feels that they have been left out.

1   **Use Post-its to allow group brainstorming.** This helps to ensure that it is not just the people who speak out most readily who are seen to be the originators of ideas.

2   **When taking oral comments from members of a group, give everyone the same opportunity.** For example, go round the whole group, giving the same time to each contribution. Next time, start with a different person, and so on.

3   **Set out to give group members equal 'air time'.** This can mean gently stemming the flow from those who have too much to say and, equally gently, encouraging the flow from those who are more reticent.

4   **Use pairs sometimes to discuss things before they report to the whole group.** This can help to increase the confidence of the more reticent members of a group. When they have already sorted out their ideas in pairs, they often find it much easier to report back to a larger group.

5   **Explore the causes of persistent 'passenger' behaviours.** Sometimes the cause can be pure laziness, but quite often there are other reasons why people may find it hard to contribute equally to a group setting. Sometimes, once these reasons are identified, you'll be able to find ways of making it easier for the people affected to input equitably to the group. For example, some learners prefer to be scribes rather than spokespersons, and so on.

6   **Allocate different tasks to respective group members.** When everyone has their own facet of the overall task to address, it becomes easier to allow equality of contribution rather than when everyone has been thinking about exactly the same thing.

Lack of clear objectives

In education and training it is increasingly accepted that objectives, or intended learning outcomes, have a vital part to play in ensuring that learning takes place successfully. This is no less true of small-group work than lectures. Moreover, the absence of clear objectives for group work is only too readily taken by learners as a signal that the group work can't really be an important part of their overall learning. The following suggestions may help you to put objectives or statements of intended learning outcomes to good use in facilitating group learning.

1   **Work out exactly what you intend each group learning session to achieve.** It is best to express this in terms of what you intend learners themselves to gain from the session. Make sure that the learning outcomes are expressed in language that learners themselves can readily understand, so that they see very clearly what they are intended to achieve.

2   **Publish the learning outcomes or objectives in advance.** This allows learners to see where any particular group session fits into the overall picture of their learning. It also helps them to see that their group learning counts towards their assessment in due course.

3   **Maintain some flexibility.** For example, it is useful to have some further objectives for any group session designed to cover matters arising from previous sessions, or to address learners' questions and needs as identified on an ongoing basis throughout a programme of study. These additional objectives can be added to the original intentions for the session and reprioritized at the start of the session if necessary.

4   **Don't just write the objectives or outcomes – use them!** State them (or display them on a slide, or issue them on a handout) at the start of each and every group session, even if it is continuing to address a list of intended outcomes which were discussed at previous sessions.

5   **Assist learners in creating their own objectives.** From time to time, ask them, 'What do you need to gain from the coming group session?', for example, giving them each a Post-it on which to jot down their replies. Then stick the Post-its on a chart (or wall, door or markerboard), and ask the group to shuffle them into an order of priority or to group them into overlapping clusters.

34

Institutional factors that can damage group work

In the preceding sections, we explored learner behaviours and facilitator behaviours that can undermine successful group learning. There are, however, further factors that are sometimes beyond the direct control of facilitators or learners. A selection of such factors is outlined below, with some suggestions about ways in which facilitators, in particular, may be able to help to solve the problems created.

- Lack of provision of suitable spaces for group learning.
- Timetabling systems which militate against group learning.
- Tensions between part-time and full-time provision.
- Institutional ethos that undervalues group learning.
- Assessment frameworks that seem to miss out the products of group learning.

Lack of provision of suitable spaces for group learning

Most institutions of tertiary level education seem to be short of teaching accommodation. There is usually reasonably adequate provision of accommodation for large-group sessions such as lectures, but the shortfall in accommodation hits group learning more severely. What can facilitators do?

1 **Use coffee bars.** Sometimes there are times when refreshment areas are quiet enough to fit in elements of group learning. It is important, however, to be really willing to move out if the staff need to clean or tidy up, otherwise there is likely to be a ruling that such areas are no longer available for informal group work.

2   **Take the group to the nearest pub!** Research shows (it is claimed) that the learning experience is significantly enhanced by such a change of environment. Be cautious, however, if the group is likely to contain members where consumption of alcohol is against their ethical codes or religion, or if the people involved simply don't enjoy going to pubs.

3   **Do a room usage audit.** It is often found that rooms which are officially 'booked' on the master timetable are only used sometimes. This data can be fed back to whoever is in charge of room bookings, and can cause considerable tightening up of the system, so releasing many additional workspaces for booking.

4   **Explore possibilities in the library.** Many libraries or learning resource centres nowadays have areas designed for group work. Sometimes there are bookable seminar rooms. Alternatively, non-quiet areas may lend themselves to drop-in group learning sessions.

5   **Ask the group to help you to solve their problem.** They may have informal learning spaces which they already use, but which you don't know about.

Timetabling systems that militate against group learning

For example, when learners are studying a wide-ranging mixture of modules, it may be just about impossible to find times when all members of a group happen to be free from other timetabled commitments. What can facilitators do?

1   **Explore possibilities of early morning or evening meetings.** Many institutions are moving towards keeping buildings open for longer, and if learners are getting a lot out of group meetings they will often make time to attend early or late meetings. Be careful, however, not to disadvantage group members who simply can't attend out of normal hours due to family or work commitments.

2   **Divert some large-group time.** When it is particularly important to make time for small-group learning, it is often possible to use a lecture slot and to arrange that several groups meet in a conventional lecture room. If the work is interesting enough, learners quickly overcome any problems of a relatively noisy environment for group meetings, especially if different groups are working concurrently on different projects.

Tensions between part-time and full-time provision

Increasingly, in large institutions, full-time learners and part-time learners are brought together for common elements of the curriculum. This is normally done to achieve economies of scale. It does, however, mean that while part-time learners may have suitably timetabled large-group sessions alongside the full-timers, they may not be able to be in the institution at all on some of the occasions when small-group follow-up sessions are being planned for the full-timers.

What can be done about these tensions?

1   **It is sometimes possible to group part-timers together.** Their group sessions can then be arranged on the days when they are in the institution for other purposes in any case. This avoids them having to make special attempts to attend outside such days. It does, however, mean that their opportunity to learn alongside full-time learners is reduced.

2   **Negotiate with the part-time learners to see whether they can meet for small-group sessions before (or after) their normal schedules.** Accommodation is usually easier to find before the day really starts, or after it finishes. This can, however, prove difficult for part-timers who have, for example, child-care commitments, which may make it difficult for them to attend at such times.

Institutional ethos that undervalues group learning

Most educational institutions attempt to place value on group learning. However, the path to effective group learning is paved with good intentions, which are sometimes not delivered in practice. It is not surprising, for example, for lecturers in universities to regard the most important parts of their teaching work as those where the highest numbers of students are involved, and small-group sessions are often treated as less critical. This leads to small-group sessions being the first thing to go when anything urgent comes up – meetings, interviews, conferences, and so on. It is not surprising in such circumstances that the attitude towards small-group work transmits itself to learners themselves, and they too soon adopt the view that their principal opportunities to learn do not arise from small-group sessions.

What can be done to change this ethos?

1   **Set out to change it.** Learners are quick to pick up signals from their teachers. When individual teachers communicate the message (for example) that the real learning will take place when the theoretical ideas from large-group sessions are applied in small-group contexts, and that it is the real learning (not the regurgitation of the theories and concepts) that will be tested in assessments, learners quickly reprioritize their thinking about the small-group work.

2   **Lead by example.** Try to avoid at all costs cancelling (or even having to reschedule) small-group sessions. Make them as 'fixed' and stable a part of learners' timetables as large-group ones.

Assessment frameworks that seem to miss out the products of group learning

Many educational institutions still place high emphasis on traditional, formal exams as the principal method of assessment. All too often, the curriculum addressed by such exams is directly linked to the content of lecture programmes and the suggested or directed reading and study undertaken by students, as briefed in their formal lectures or course handbooks. Small-group learning can end up being relegated to the status of 'icing on the cake', rather than something much more important.

What can individual learning facilitators do about this? Here are some possibilities.

1   **Include some parts of the curriculum that will only be addressed in small-group situations.** Make these explicit to learners. Tell them what proportion of the overall curriculum they represent, and include an appropriate fraction of questions, in the exams themselves, that relate to the learning achievements that are intended to be realized through group learning.

2   **Express intended learning outcomes for group learning alongside those for other learning situations.** Then devise assessment criteria for the group learning outcomes in the same way as for any other learning format. This helps to communicate to learners that group learning is being regarded as just as important as any other kind of learning, and will contribute to assessment in the same kinds of ways as lectures, practical work, and so on.

35

Conflict in group work

Much has been written about the stages that are quite normal in group work. For example, it is common for groups to progress through stages of 'forming, storming, norming, and conforming' – not necessarily in one particular order! The following suggestions may help you to minimize the dangers associated with conflict in group work, and to maximize the benefits that can be drawn from people who sometimes disagree.

1   **Legitimize conflict.** It is important to acknowledge that people don't have to agree all of the time, and to open up agreed processes by which areas of disagreement can be explored and resolved (or be agreed to remain areas of disagreement). Ensure, however, that the groups have ground rules for conflict resolution, so that they strive to avoid slanging matches and power games.

2   **Establish the causes of conflict.** When conflict has broken out in a group, it is easy for the root causes to become subsumed in an escalation of feeling. It can be productive to backtrack to the exact instance that initiated the conflict and to analyse it further.

3   **Encourage groups to put the conflict into written words.** Writing up the issues, problems or areas of disagreement on a flipchart or markerboard can help to get them out of people's systems. Conflict feelings are often much stronger when the conflict is still bottled up and has not yet been clearly expressed or acknowledged. When something is 'up on the wall', it often looks less daunting, and a person who felt strongly about it may be more satisfied. The 'on the wall' issues can be returned to later when the group has had more time to think about them.

4   **Establish the ownership of the conflict.** Who feels it? Who is being affected by it? Distinguish between individual issues and ones that affect the whole group.

5   **Distinguish between people, actions and opinions.** When unpacking the causes of conflict in a group situation, it is useful to focus on actions and principles. Try to resolve any actions that proved to cause conflict. Try to agree principles. If the conflict is caused by different opinions, it can help to accept people's entitlement to their opinions and leave it open to people to reconsider their opinions if and when they feel ready to do so.

6   **Use conflict creatively.** It can be useful to use brainstorming to obtain a wider range of views or a broader range of possible actions that can be considered by the group. Sometimes, the one or two strong views, which may have caused conflict in a group, look much more reasonable when the full range of possibilities is aired and areas of agreement are found to be closer than they seemed to be.

7   **Capture the learning from conflict.** When conflict has occurred, it can be beneficial to ask everyone to decide on the constructive things they have learnt about themselves from the conflict and to agree on principles, which the whole group can apply to future activities, to minimize the damage from similar causes of conflict arising again.

8   **Refuse to allow conflict to destroy group work.** You may wish sometimes to tell groups that achievement of consensus is an aim or a norm or, alternatively, you may wish to ask groups to establish only the extent of the consensus they achieve.

9   **Consider arbitration processes.** When conflict is absolutely unresolvable, the facilitator may need to set up a 'court of appeal' for desperate situations. The fact that such a process is available often helps groups to sort out their own problems without having to resort to it.

10 **Make it OK to escape.** When people know that they can get out of an impossible situation, they don't feel trapped and, in fact, are more likely to work their own way out of the conflict. It can be useful to allow people to drop out of a group and move into another one, but only as a last resort. Beware of the possible effects of someone who is seen as a conflict generator entering a group that has so far worked without conflict!

36

Gender issues in group work

When problems occur in groups due to gender issues, they can be felt more deeply than problems arising from almost any other cause. The following suggestions may help you to avoid some problems of this sort from arising in the first place, or to alert group members themselves to the potential problems, so that they can work round them in their own group work.

1   **Think about gender when forming groups.** There are advantages and disadvantages for single sex groups, depending on the balance of the sexes, and other issues including culturally sensitive ones. In some cultures, females may be much happier, for religious reasons, working in single sex groups. However, in other cases it may be helpful in terms of future employment to gently encourage them to get used to working with members of the opposite sex.

2   **Try to avoid gender domination of groups.** This can happen because of majority gender composition of groups. If this is inevitable, because of the overall gender balance of the whole group, try to manage group composition so that minority participants don't feel isolated. If it is unavoidable, address the issue directly when setting ground rules.

3   **Decide when single gender groups might be more appropriate.** For group work on gender sensitive issues, such as child abuse, it can be best to set out to form single sex groups.

4   **Require appropriate behaviour.** For group work to be effective, all participants need to behave in a professional way with standards that would be expected in an effective working environment. Outlaw sexist or offensive behaviour and emphasize that one person's 'joke' or 'tease' can be another person's humiliation.

5   **Decide when to stick with existing group compositions.** When a set of groups is working well, without any gender-related or other problems, don't just change the group composition without a good reason.

6   **Set ground rules for talking and listening.** It can be useful to agree on ground rules that will ensure that all group participants (irrespective of gender) are heard, and not talked down to or over by other participants.

7   **Avoid setting up excessive competition between male groups and female groups.** When there are gender-specific groups, don't egg a group of one gender on, by saying words to the effect, 'Come on, you can do better than them' when referring to groups of the other gender.

8   **Be sensitive about role assignment.** For example, try to raise awareness about the dangers of tasks being allocated within groups on the basis of gender stereotypes, such as typing or making arrangements being handled by females and 'heavy' work by males.

9   **Alert groups to be sensitive to leadership issues.** It is often the case that, for example, male members of groups may automatically see themselves as stronger contenders to lead the group than their female counterparts and put themselves forward. When group members are aware that this is an issue, they are more likely to agree on a more democratic process for deciding who will lead an activity or who will report back the outcomes.

10 **Avoid sexual preference oppression.** When it is known that group participants have different sexual preferences from the majority of the group, there is a tendency for them to be oppressed in one way or another by the rest of the group. It can be delicate to raise this issue in general briefings, and it may be best to respond to it as a facilitator when it is seen to be likely to occur.

Chapter 6   Assessing group learning

Assessing group learning is one of the most difficult tasks to do well. This is at least partly because there are two dimensions of group work that may be involved in assessment: the product of the group work, and the processes which contributed to its development. However, the most important single issue is often the tricky matter of establishing the levels of contribution of respective members to both product and process alike. There are several approaches to the task, each with its advantages and disadvantages. There is probably no single ideal way to assess group learning, and you will need to work out the balance of the pros and cons of each of the approaches outlined below in the context of your own work.

Rather than present a series of tips on this complex topic, various overlapping possibilities are presented below, each with a number of pros and cons, based on the work by Sally Brown. Notice that even in a given context, the pros and cons listed can conflict with each other – groups can behave in very different ways. The possibilities explored in this chapter are summarized below, then each is discussed in more detail.

37   Take the simplest path – just use the same group mark for all involved.
38   Divide and concur – divide up the assessed group task and assess each component separately.
39   Add differentials – give a mark for the overall group product, but negotiate differentials between group members.
40   Add contribution marks – award a mark for the product of the group, and ask group members to peer-assess an additional mark for their contribution.
41   Add more tasks – award an equal mark to each member for the product of the group task, then add individual assessed tasks for each member of the group.
42   Test them orally – award all group members the same mark for their product, but add an individual viva (oral exam).
43   Test them in writing – allow the group mark for the product to stand, but add a separate related assessment component to an exam.

37

Take the simplest path
– just use the same group mark for all involved

Advantages

- This approach is easy to manage. It is the least time consuming of all the options available.

- When group members know in advance that they will all receive equal credit for their work, they may be more willing to try to ensure for themselves that their contribution is equal.

- It is worth considering if it is primarily the product of the group learning that is to be assessed and not the processes leading up to this product.

- It is useful if the assessment doesn't contribute to summative assessment, as then learners are unlikely to be too concerned at their respective contributions to the work of the group not being assessed.

- It can be appropriate if the task is fairly small, and it is felt that it would not be worth the time it would take to assess process as well as product.

- Giving the same group mark is appropriate if the members of the group work well together and are in small cohesive groups.

Disadvantages

- Giving the same mark for all can be perceived as unfair, encouraging passengers, giving no bonus for excellence.

- This approach does not acknowledge the importance of group processes and, therefore, learners may not try to engage in the processes as seriously as they do when it is known by them that process will count alongside product.

- Groups may allow passengers on the first occasion this approach is used, but become resentful of them in future assessed group tasks, leading to dysfunctional groups later.

38

Divide and concur
– divide up the assessed group task, and assess each component separately

Advantages

- This can help groups to avoid disagreement, as everyone knows that their assessment will depend primarily on their own work.

- This approach enables individuals to shine, and to know that the success of their work will be attributed directly to them.

- This can work well when it is intended to assess group product rather than process, and when it is relatively easy to divide the product into separate, equal components.

- This approach can be a way of ensuring that everyone shares the work of the group, each doing their own part of it.

- Each of the members of the group carries responsibility for their own part of the overall work.

Disadvantages

- It can be difficult to find equivalent tasks for all, and disputes may break out if some members of the group feel that they have been burdened with more demanding tasks than others.

- The overall assessment load is increased, and it can be difficult to balance assessment decisions across the group, particularly if some members were set more demanding tasks than others.

- Splitting up the work of the group goes against promoting interaction, and group processes may be regarded as being unimportant by group members.

- Problems can arise when individuals don't pull their weight, and where passengers hinder other members of the group developing their own elements of group product.

39

Add differentials
– give a mark for the overall group product, but negotiate differentials between group members

For example, in a group of four members, award the group product 65 per cent, then ask the group to divide up (4 x 65 per cent) according to the way they feel the work was shared. You may need to decide whether to leave the differentials entirely to the group, or to make a ruling (for example) that a maximum differential should be 20 per cent.

Advantages
- This approach is perceived to be fair and to place value on individual contribution to the work of the group.

- This approach gives ownership to the group of the method of differentiation of the assessment of their overall work.

- It is a method of assessing process as well as product, and causing the members of the group to reflect on their level of contribution to the overall product of the group.

- When group members know that their contribution is going to be assessed, they may be more willing to set out to contribute fully to the work of the group.

- The onus of awarding credit for group processes is taken away from the assessor, who may not in any case be in a good position to estimate the equivalence of contribution of members of the group.

Disadvantages

- This approach needs a mature group to achieve consensus, and can be found very intimidating to groups whose members don't know each other very well.

- This approach can result in everyone just agreeing to have the same mark, while causing internal resentments to build up inside the groups where contributions have not been equivalent, destabilizing the group in future collaborative work together.

- There can be substantial variations between groups in the ways they handle the task of distributing the credit for the products of their work, with some groups just making minor adjustments to the overall score, and other groups giving zero for a passenger and splitting up the remaining marks between the members who claim to have done the work.

- If a particular score hovers close to an important borderline (such as that between an award of 'credit' or 'distinction', or a degree classification boundary), there could be the temptation to employ the differentials strategically, to get as many members of the group as possible above particular borderlines, possibly at the expense of one member's award.

40

Add contribution marks
– award a mark for the product of the group, and
ask group members to peer-assess an additional
mark for their contribution

In other words, for example, award each member of the group 65 marks for
the product, and ask them to award each other member of the group between
0 and 10 for the extent to which they contributed to the work.

Advantages
- This approach enables group members to feel justice is being sought in the
  assessment of their work.
- It encourages them to value process as well as outcome, and gives the message that process is regarded as being important.
- The group members themselves may be the only people who can, if they
  are willing, make a realistic assessment of each other's contributions to their
  overall work.
- It can promote positive group behaviour, when group members are aware
  in advance that everyone in the group will be making an assessment of
  contribution to the work of the group.
- A great deal of learning about process can be engendered by involving learners in well-organized peer-assessment.

Disadvantages
- Learners may turn round and say, 'It's your job, not mine, to assess my
  work'.

- Training and practice is needed before group members enter into peer-assessment, as they may be reluctant to mark down peers and may agree to award each other equal (or maximum) marks for the process component of their work.

- It takes careful organization to get each member to record peer-assessment scores for their colleagues, for example, by secret ballot.

- Members of some groups may be quite unwilling to make this kind of internal peer-assessment, and may find it threatening to the bonding that may have occurred during the group work.

41

Add more tasks
– award an equal mark to each member for the product of the group task, then add individual assessed tasks for each member of the group

Advantages
- This can be a way to accommodate the diversity of group members, and can allow them to take responsibility for allocating the additional tasks between group members.
- It minimizes the amount passengers can benefit.
- It can offer scope for individuals to shine, and to get full credit for their individual strengths as demonstrated through the products of their separate tasks.

Disadvantages
- This can make considerably more work for assessors.
- Deciding equivalent additional tasks can be difficult.
- A group that plays to its strengths in the additional tasks will receive more credit than one that plays to its weaknesses. However, the learning payoff will be better when groups decide to play to weaknesses, so the danger amounts to penalizing groups that decide to go for high learning payoff.
- Reverting to individual work after group work may be seen by group members to undermine the perceived value of their group processes.

42

Test them orally
– award all group members the same mark for their product, but add an individual viva (oral exam)

Advantages

- This enables assessors to test individual participation. Whether the viva is done with the group as a whole, or with individual members separately, it is usually fairly easy to establish a reasonably accurate impression of whether the group members contributed equally to the work of the group.

- The approach enables an element of differentiation, allowing the group members who may have done more than their share of the work to be rewarded.

- It is seen to be fair by group members, and if they know that this external check on their processes will take place in due course, they may be more willing to seek to contribute equally to the work.

- Group members will be more willing to revisit what they did as a group, and to revise what they learnt from the process, when they know that they could be asked to explain it again in the context of a viva.

Disadvantages

- Vivas can be stressful. Some group members may not give an accurate impression of their contribution, either by (through shyness or modesty) underplaying their contribution, or by some members being able to 'fake good' in the viva when in fact their contribution was not good.

- This approach makes more work for assessors.

- Subsequent groups (or group members) may have an unfair advantage if the questions used at the viva 'leak out' during the round of vivas, allowing them to rehearse their replies to the questions.

- To be fair, the same questions need to be asked of each group (or each group member), but the best questions to use usually emerge gradually over a series of vivas.

43

Test them in writing
– allow the group mark for the product to stand, but add a separate related assessment component to an exam

Advantages
- This approach makes it more difficult for most passengers to evade justice and is perceived to be fair.
- It can allow the most deserving individuals the opportunity to shine.
- Knowing that group work remains on the exam agenda causes learners to include such work in their revision for exams, causing them to deepen their own learning by reflecting further on the group work.

Disadvantages
- The exam may not be testing the same kinds of skills as the group work itself, and may unduly reward candidates who happen to be skilled at written exams.
- More marking will be involved.
- Some candidates are able to 'fake good' in written answers relating to the group work, even though they may not have contributed well to the work.

Further Reading

A wide range of literature exists on group behaviour, including texts on facilitating group learning. The following selection of this literature will be found useful for readers wishing to further explore the ways in which groups can be helped in contexts of group learning.

Beaty, Liz and McGill, Ian (1992) *Action Learning: a practitioner's guide*, Kogan Page, London, UK

Brandes, Donna and Norris, John (1998) *The Gamester's Handbook 3*, Stanley Thornes, Cheltenham, UK

Brandes, Donna and Phillips, Howard (1990) *The Gamester's Handbook 1*, Stanley Thornes, Cheltenham, UK

Brandes, Donna and Phillips, Howard (1990) *The Gamester's Handbook 2*, Stanley Thornes, Cheltenham, UK

Brown, R (1988) *Group Processes: Dynamics within and between groups*, Blackwell, Oxford, UK

Brown, Sally (1996) The Art of Teaching in Small Groups – 1 *The New Academic*, **5** (3), SEDA, Birmingham, UK

Brown, Sally (1997) The Art of Teaching in Small Groups – 2 *The New Academic*, **6** (1), SEDA, Birmingham, UK

Brown, Sally and Race, Phil (1997) *Staff Development in Action*, SEDA Paper 100, SEDA Publications, Birmingham, UK

Gibbs, Graham (1994) *Learning in Teams: A student manual*, Oxford Centre for Staff and Learning Development, Oxford, UK

Gibbs, Graham (1995) *Learning in Teams: A tutor manual*, Oxford Centre for Staff and Learning Development, Oxford, UK

Gibbs, Graham, Habeshaw, Trevor and Jaques, David (1992) *Teaching More Students 3: Discussion with more students*, Oxford Centre for Staff and Learning Development, Oxford, UK

Habeshaw, Sue and Steeds, Di (1987) *53 Interesting Communication Exercises for Science Students*, TES, Bristol, UK

Hardingham, Alison (1998) *Working in Teams*, IPD Books, London, UK

Heron, John (1989) *The Facilitator's Handbook*, Kogan Page, London, UK

Jaques, David (2000) *Learning in Groups*, 3rd edn, Kogan Page, London, UK

Johnson, D W and Johnson, F P (1991) *Joining Together: Group theory and group skills*, Prentice Hall, New Jersey, US

Leigh, David (1996) *Designing and Delivering Training for Groups*, Kogan Page, London, UK

Thorley, Lin and Gregory, Roy (1994) *Using Group based Learning in Higher Education*, Kogan Page, London, UK

Tiberius, Richard G (1999) *Small Group Teaching: A trouble-shooting guide*, Kogan Page, London, UK

Zander, A (1982) *Making Groups Effective*, Jossey-Bass, San Francisco, US

Index

Visit Kogan Page on-line

Comprehensive information on
Kogan Page titles

Features include

- complete catalogue listings,
  including book reviews and
  descriptions

- on-line discounts on a variety
  of titles

- special monthly promotions

- information and discounts on
  NEW titles and BESTSELLING titles

- a secure shopping basket facility
  for on-line ordering

- infoZones, with links and
  information on specific areas of
  interest

PLUS everything you need to know
about KOGAN PAGE

http://www.kogan-page.co.uk